Teacher Written Commentary
in Second Language Writing Classrooms

 Michigan Series on Teaching Multilingual Writers

Series Editors
Diane Belcher (Georgia State University) and
Jun Liu (University of Arizona)

Available titles in the series

Treatment of Error in Second Language Student Writing
  Dana R. Ferris

Peer Response in Second Language Writing Classrooms
  Jun Liu & Jette G. Hansen

Critical Academic Writing and Multilingual Students
  A. Suresh Canagarajah

Controversies in Second Language Writing:
Dilemmas and Decisions in Research and Instruction
  Christine Pearson Casanave

Connecting Reading and Writing in Second Language
Writing Instuction
  Alan Hirvela

Genre and Second Language Writing
  Ken Hyland

Teacher Written Commentary in Second Language Writing Classrooms

Lynn M. Goldstein

The Monterey Institute of International Studies

 Michigan Series on Teaching Multilingual Writers

Ann Arbor
THE UNIVERSITY OF MICHIGAN PRESS

Library of Congress Cataloging-in-Publication Data

Goldstein, Lynn M.
    Teacher written commentary in second language writing classrooms / Lynn M. Goldstein
        p.   cm.—(Michigan series on teaching multilingual writers)
    Includes bibliographical references and index.
    ISBN 0-472-03016-7 (pbk. : alk paper)
        1. Rhetoric—Study and teaching (Higher) 2. Editing. 3. Teacher-student relationships.
    I. Title. II. Series.

    P53.27.G65   2005
    808'.0428'0711—dc22   2004062146

Acknowledgments

Grateful acknowledgment is given to the following authors, publishers, and individuals for permission to reprint previously published or copyrighted materials.

Len Fox of Brooklyn College for methodology of error correction.

John Hedgcock for permission to use adapted material from ED 560, class assignment.

Robert Kohls for comments, suggestions, or feedback to students.

Elizabeth (Mason) Monaco for data collected from the ES 325 class at the Monterey Institute of International Studies.

Newsweek, Inc. for "Helping the Needy Crack the Tax Code," by Robert Burke, from *Newsweek,* 4/26/04, © 2004 Newsweek, Inc. All rights reserved. Reprinted by permission.

Thomson Learning for material from *Learning About Language Assessment: Dilemmas, Decisions and Directions,* 1st edition BAILEY. © 1998. Reprinted with permission of Heinle, a division of Thomson Learning: www.thomsonrights.com. Fax 800-730-2215.

To the following second language students who allowed their material to appear in this book: Bingo, Chu Hua, Dang, Gin, Hoshiko, Jan, Jin, Lin, Linh, Marigrace, Masaki, Mei, Melik, Pilar, Sam, Takara, Thu, Trahn, and Zohre. [These are all pseudonyms.]

To the following second language writing teachers and TESOL graduate students who allowed their feedback and reflections to appear in this book: Maryam Al Hinai, Kelley Calvert, Bridget DeYager, Denise Egri, Victor Enriquez, Len Fox, Stuart Landers, Ellie Mason Monaco, Charles Mueller, Anne O'Farrell, John Thorpe, and Marion Wang. (All of their work appears under pseudonyms in the book.)

Every effort has been made to contact the copyright holders for permission to reprint borrowed material. We regret any oversights that may have occurred and will rectify them in future printings of this book.

Contents

Series Foreword by Diane Belcher and Jun Liu   ix

Preface   xi

Introduction   1

1. **Understanding the Role of Context in Teacher Commentary and Student Revision Response   9**

    Understanding How Institutional and Programmatic Context May Affect Commentary
        Providing Commentary within Specific Institutional and Programmatic Constraints

    Taking Student and Teacher Factors into Account as They Shape Context and Commentary

    An Overview of Context

2. **Establishing Effective Communication between Teacher and Student   26**

    Avoiding Appropriation: Understanding and Responding within the Student's Rhetorical Context

    Listening to Teachers: Educating Students about Teacher Commentary

    Listening to Students: Educating Teachers about Student Preferences, Needs, and Difficulties

    Conclusion

3. **Understanding the Nature of Effective Commentary   61**

    Helping Students Read Their Writing Critically and Communicate Areas on Which They Would Like Feedback

    Determining What to Comment On

    Commenting on Writing Processes

    Shaping Teacher Commentary

    Addressing What Students Need to Learn about Writing and about Texts

    Putting It All Together: Planning for Response

4. Reflective Teaching and Teacher Research   103

Reflective Teaching

Possibilities for Reflection
   The Nature of What Is and Is Not Commented On
   The Nature of Comments: What Shape Do My Comments
      Take?
   The Interaction between Commentary and Revision

Other Areas for Research

Sharing Research

Conducting Sound Research

Reporting Research

Conclusion

5. Educating Pre- and In-Service Second Language Composition Teachers   125

Preliminaries: Process, Product, and Genre

Pre-Service Teachers: Learning about Response as a Whole
   Class

Choosing Students/Texts for Individual Practice for Pre-
   Service Teachers

The Response Assignment

Giving Teachers Feedback on Their Written Responses

In-Service Teachers: Learning about Response while Teaching

Summary

References   148
Subject Index   155
Author Index   161

Series Foreword

There are many reasons why a series such as ours, on teaching multilingual writers, should include a book focused exclusively on teacher written feedback. It is difficult to teach writing for any length of time without arriving at the realization that the classroom is only one of the instructional sites for the teaching of writing. Equally, if not more, critical may be the instruction that takes place in the margins of our students' papers (Hyland, 1998; Leki, 1990). Yet, while many of us may intuitively feel that teacher written response is crucial to the success of any composition class, to say that the writing of commentary on student paper is—for some of us—*not* one of our favorite activities is no doubt an understatement. Not only can responding to student texts be exceedingly time consuming, but given the always real possibility that some number of subsequent student drafts will show little or no evidence of having benefited from our feedback, responding can also be a seemingly thankless, frustrating task. Even, and perhaps especially, those of us who have taught writing for many years stay on the lookout for more effective and efficient ways to respond to student texts.

In Lynn Goldstein's *Teacher Written Commentary in Second Language Writing Classrooms*, it is clear that the author understands teachers' needs and feelings well, not just because of her obvious familiarity with teacher feedback research, as a consumer and a producer of it, but also as a result of her decades of work in the field of second language (L2) writing as a teacher and teacher-trainer. Through the lens of her substantial experience, which has provided her with a fund of vivid examples of the teacher/student interface (or lack thereof), Goldstein sorts out for us the not always clear-cut findings of recent feedback research and helps us appreciate their implications with regard to a number of longstanding teacher feedback dilemmas. Among the problems that Goldstein addresses are how to attend to product without slighting process, how to intervene in process without appropriating product, how to facilitate student comprehension and use of teacher feedback while promoting student independence, and how to respond relatively efficiently yet remain attentive to individual student needs. These are challenging issues in any writing class but are decidedly more so when a teacher must consider the varied cultural and education backgrounds and proficiency levels of multilingual writers, who may have never thought of writing as a process, of teachers as facilitators, or of written comments, which they may or may not be able to decode, as invitations to revise.

Goldstein does not promise to solve all the responding problems of L2 writing teachers—to greatly accelerate our "marking up" time or radically transform our students' feedback attitudes and revision behaviors. What she does instead is provide the tools for us to reflect on and fine-tune our responding (i.e., communication) strategies, tools that may, through our own informed use of them, make our intuitions about the potential value of written feedback more than wishful thinking.

References

Hyland, F. (1998). The impact of teacher written feedback on individual writers. *Journal of Second Language Writing, 7*, 255–286.

Leki, I. (1990). Coaching from the margins: Issue in written response. In B. Kroll (Ed.), *Second language writing: Research insights for the classroom* (pp. 57–68). Cambridge, UK: Cambridge University Press.

Diane Belcher,
Georgia State University

Jun Liu,
University of Arizona

Preface

In 1977, I taught my first writing class, literally on a wing and a prayer. I had an MA degree, a bit of teaching experience, but I had never taught writing. While I would like to be able to report I did everything right, at least when it comes to written feedback, I did everything wrong. I responded to everything at once, I responded as though I had a template with which I would measure the "success" and effectiveness of each student's writing, and I wasn't often systematic or text-specific with my commentary. Quickly I became discomforted. I reached for everything I could find to read, poured over student textbooks, and talked to colleagues. However, at that time, I found only a little in the L2 writing field that could guide my commenting practices and only somewhat more in the L1 writing field. Over the years, I have continued to search, read, and talk while experimenting and refining my practices. This book represents that journey and what I have learned about teacher written commentary and student revision over the almost 30 years of being involved with different facets of teaching L2 writing, educating L2 writing teachers, directing L2 writing programs, and conducting research about L2 writing.

There are many people who have been enormously helpful and influential over these years. My first professional "home" was LaGuardia Community College, where my colleagues were always generous in sharing their time and ideas about effective pedagogy. Here they trusted a novice teacher. I am grateful for that trust and generosity beyond words as it set the stage for all that has come since. To all my friends and colleagues at LaGuardia during that wonderful time, I offer my heartfelt thanks. Next, at Hunter College, Anne Raimes provided the support and trust that allowed me to explore my teaching and to take on administrative responsibilities for running the English for Bilingual Students program and working with adjunct teachers on teacher development. Here I began to learn how to share my explorations with others. At my current "home," the Monterey Institute of International Studies, where I have been for the past 18 years, I have been gifted with wonderful, supportive colleagues. Early on, I was allowed to create and then direct the writing program for graduate students in policy studies and business and to develop and teach a course for TESOL graduate students on the teaching of L2 writing. These have been seminal experiences for me, through which I have learned so much. Here, too, I began my research into teacher feedback and student revision, some of which has been supported by the generosity of the Institute's Mark Awards.

Far and wide I have been influenced by, educated by, and supported by a whole community of teachers and scholars committed to understanding L2 writers and writing. To the following people go my thanks: Diane Belcher, Elaine Brooks, Cherry Campbell, Joan Carson, Joanne Cavallaro, Susan Conrad, Melinda Erickson, John Hedgcock, Robbie Kantor, Anne Katz, Robert Kohls, Ilona Leki, Jun Liu, and Tony Silva. Some of you have read pages of this book or my research and writing and offered cogent and helpful feedback, while others have carried on conversations with me over the years about the many facets of L2 writing from which I have learned and benefited greatly.

Thanks also are due to my students: L2 writers, along with whom and from whom I have learned about feedback and revision; L2 writers who generously gave of their time and work, allowing me to carry out research to learn about teacher commentary and student revision; and my graduate students who have always pushed me to best provide them with the tools to carry out effective commentary practices with their L2 writing students. Many of my L2 writing students and graduate students have over the years also generously shared their work with me for research and teaching purposes, and I am thankful for being able to use this work (all names have been changed to pseudonyms) throughout this book.

Finally, this book and my professional journey would not be possible without the love and support of my family. To my husband, Dennis McCarthy, heartfelt thanks and love for your unerring support and your pride in my accomplishments, and to my children, Daniel and Matthew, love and thanks for your patience and understanding when on those occasions I was writing and could not come to your baseball and basketball games. To my mother, Corrine Sharcoff, you saw the beginning of this journey and this book, but died before its completion. From the beginning, long before I could read or write, you shared your joys of writing, writing stories to read to me and writing down my stories as I told them to you. Your love, your support, and your faith in me remain.

Introduction

In 1977, I began teaching second language writing at a community college in New York City. Nothing in the courses that I had taken for my MA degree or any of my few previous teaching experiences had prepared me for the challenges that would lie ahead. In an attempt to do my best for my students, I read everything I could find on teaching composition to multilingual writers, and I looked at every textbook I could locate. There was not a lot at that time about multilingual writers, so I relied heavily on the L1 literature. Additionally, there were only a few textbooks for multilingual writers, and they mostly focused on sentence-level and paragraph concerns in a very static, decontextualized, and linear manner.

My students wanted grammar lessons, and they wanted me to correct all of their sentence-level errors. While I did not deny their concerns and can see to this day the legitimacy of working with students on sentence-level errors (see Ferris, 2002, for sound arguments for doing so), I just knew that this couldn't be the only aspect of writing to which my students and I should be attending. After all, they were saying something when they wrote, and it seemed that in some way I should be attending to *what* they had to say as well as *how* they were saying it using the rhetorical resources available to them.

By my second semester of teaching, emboldened by some of the literature I was reading in the L1 composition field and heartened by discussions with colleagues with similar sentiments, I embarked on a journey to determine what would be the best and most effective ways to respond to the content and rhetoric of my students' writing so that they could become more effective and more independent writers. That 25-year journey has led me here, to this volume on how to provide effective written commentary to multilingual writers.

I have looked at the issue of teacher response from many angles. My journey has encompassed not only my own teaching of second language writing but also my research into the relationship between teacher commentary and student revision, my teaching courses on the teaching of writing to ESL writers for in- and pre-service teachers, and my work with in-service teachers on their responding practices in writing programs I have directed.

Over time I have discovered that all teachers—pre-service and in-service alike—grapple with how best to provide effective written feedback to their students' texts. Interestingly, despite the paradigm shift in L1 writing that Maxine Hairston wrote of in 1982, and despite the attention within the L2 literature on "process" approaches to writing, the teachers I work with bring little from their personal experiences as first and second language writers that they feel inform them, in positive ways, of how best to respond in writing to their students' work. At the beginning of my course on the teaching of writing to L2 writers, I ask my student teachers to reflect on and discuss their memories about learning how to write in both their first language and, for those who have learned an additional language or English as an additional language, on learning to write in a language other than one's first. One student teacher wrote, "I don't remember learning how to read or write, except for a few dim memories of learning cursive in the third grade." Over the years, many student teachers have also said they received little writing instruction and that when they did have writing instruction, it focused on the five-paragraph essay, rhetorical models, and sentence-level concerns. In discussing written feedback they have received on their writing, many student teachers are quick to list what they do not like, and many have numerous examples of receiving little to no useful feedback on their papers. This is not to say that I have not worked with student teachers that have received effective instruction and feedback but that many of them have not experienced sound models of effective written commentary from which to draw on when providing commentary to their own students. In fact, because feedback and revision is so central to helping L2 writers become more effective writers, I spend approximately a quarter of our class time over the semester with my student teachers on the issues and practices of giving effective commentary. And what I see each and every semester are the difficulties graduate students experience as they work on their feedback. I believe that almost every one of them would say that learning how to give effective feedback is the most time-consuming and most difficult aspect of teaching L2 writing. Moreover, when I work with in-service teachers, I hear the same refrain—that providing useful feedback to their students is extraordinarily difficult and time consuming (Ferris, Pezone, Tade, & Tinti, 1997).

This volume in the Michigan Series on Teaching Multilingual Writers identifies the issues to which teachers need to attend and the practices they need to employ in providing written commentary on rhetoric and content in their students' writing. In turn, the book fills a gap that exists in the literature, as there is no single source that gives as in-depth treatment of the issues and the range of practices within teacher written commentary and that focuses solely on issues of rhetoric and content in multilingual writers' texts. While I would not claim that we can necessarily reduce the time involved in providing effective written commentary, I do believe that the issues and practices to be discussed within this volume will enable teachers to provide written commentary that will help their students become more effective and more independent writers in English. In addition to teachers of multilingual writers, the audience for whom this book is intended includes teacher educators and supervisors of in-service teachers who are looking for an in-depth discussion of teacher commentary to use with their pre- and in-service teachers and researchers who are looking to identify which issues and practices need examination.

In fact, with the exception of a few articles published in the mid- to late 1980s (see Radecki & Swales, 1988; Zamel, 1985), research on written commentary really did not get much attention until the 1990s. The research that has since ensued has addressed three main areas of inquiry: (1) students' perceptions of and attitudes toward teacher written commentary, including students' self-reports of how they use commentary when revising; (2) the ways teachers comment on their students' writing; and (3) the relationship between teacher commentary and student revision. While this book will use findings from the research, whenever appropriate, to support pedagogical practices, it should be noted that many issues inherent in commentary have yet to be addressed or adequately addressed in the research literature (see Goldstein, 2001, for a full discussion of the shortcomings in the present body of research). For this reason, suggested practices are also grounded in the experiences of the author and of others from whom I have been fortunate to learn.

Why Should Teachers Provide Written Commentary

Before turning to the chapters that follow, since providing written commentary is time consuming and labor intensive, we might ask what can be gained by providing written commentary to students on their texts. I have certainly heard teachers complain that their efforts go "unrewarded"—that is, that their students ignore their feedback or misuse their feedback and that their students' texts are not much improved.

My experience and that of other teachers I have worked with, however, argues otherwise. From observing my own practices as well as those of others whose students do use their commentary and whose writing does show the positive effects of appropriate commentary, I believe the key is the effectiveness of the commentary provided and the quality of the communication between teachers and students about the teachers' commentary and the students' revisions (Leki, 1993). While I will discuss in great detail throughout the book what needs to be considered in providing effective commentary, my discussion here will focus on some considerations that support the practice of providing written commentary.

Despite claims to the contrary (Krashen, 1984), most writing teachers agree that students do not become more proficient writers just by reading and writing. Students need some form of feedback that helps them see how others are reading their writing and what revisions might strengthen their writing. There are many justifications for this. First, in most cases, writing is fundamentally a social act involving the author and readers (an audience) (Ede & Lundsford, 1984; Ferris & Hedgcock, 1998). All writers need to learn what their audiences expect and whether or not their writing is being read in the ways they would like by their audience(s). Even proficient writers attest to asking others to read and comment on their writing. A range of readers are available to students: peers, professors in the disciplines, friends, writing center tutors, and second language writing course teachers. Each audience can bring something unique to the role of audience, and all can provide a felt sense of audience. In addition, while each audience may be able to point out where a text is not accomplishing what the author would like and why, L2 writing teachers can *explain* why and provide strategies for remedying these problems, something that other readers who are not trained to do so and or are not as experienced in doing so may not be able to accomplish as well or as readily.

This felt sense of audience is particularly important when we consider the interactive nature of reading and writing (Ferris & Hedgcock, 1998; Leki, 1993; Reid, 1993). Students need to learn that the words they inscribe on paper are not static and that meaning resides not only in these words but also in what the audience brings to the reading of these words. This can only be understood if students get feedback from readers, feedback that shows writers where what they have intended has been achieved and where their texts may have fallen short of their intentions and goals. The teacher's feedback can play a critical role in providing this feedback by helping students see mismatches between intentions and readings. Such feedback can also inform students about how to solve these mismatches.

Further support for the teacher's role in providing feedback can be seen in discussions of language awareness and discussions of working with those more "expert" than oneself. One way to envision language awareness is to see it "in terms of increasing (raising) the amount of conscious knowledge in each individual through new and explicit input from teachers" (James & Garrett, 1991, p. 6). Teacher written commentary can provide this new and explicit input that makes students aware of what is and is not "working" in their texts. In addition, Liu and Hansen (2002), in their volume on peer responding, point out the benefits gained when students work with peers within Vygotsky's zone of proximal development. Working with a more knowledgeable person, however, does not need to be limited to peers. Teacher written commentary is also an effective means by which a student can work with and gain from working with a more knowledgeable person. As Grabe and Kaplan (1996) state in discussing the application of Vygotsky's theories to the teaching and learning of L2 writing, "the student learns to write by working with a more knowledgeable person on the skills and knowledge needed to perform specific purposeful actions through a kind of apprenticeship . . . students gradually learn through feedback on writing" (pp. 242–243).

Process approaches to the teaching and learning of L2 writing also argue for teacher intervention and feedback at key points within the process. (As I will discuss in later chapters, like others [e.g., Grabe & Kaplan, 1996], my notion of process encompasses attention to both process and product.) One aspect of a process approach involves students writing successive drafts as they move closer to producing a text that achieves their goals and intentions for that draft and also meets the needs of the audience within whatever rhetorical context they are writing. These successive drafts are informed by the reactions of readers. Teachers, as "expert" readers, are able to help students identify what they need to learn in terms of effective processes and in terms of the knowledge of what is required when generating these drafts and to arrive at the most successful final product possible.

Teacher commentary is also supported by the notion that students learn more effectively when they learn through contexts they themselves have created. It is certainly possible to teach students about audience, purpose, organization, and development by analyzing texts written by others. Nonetheless, many teachers I have worked with have found that students have difficulty applying what they have learned from text analysis without also examining how effectively they are addressing rhetorical concerns in their own writing. Here, again, teacher feedback is crucial to helping students see what is and is not working within their own texts and is crucial in helping students identify and enact strategies for solving rhetorical problems in their texts.

Some may argue that teacher written commentary is a less effective means of giving feedback and that oral feedback through conferences is the preferred approach. Those who espouse this view believe that conferences provide for better communication between teacher and student than teacher written commentary. While anecdotally some teachers may lay claim to better communication in conferences, in fact no research shows this to be true. My own research on teacher-student conferences (Goldstein & Conrad, 1990), revealed that conferences were not an inherently effective means by which feedback could be given and adopted. Many factors affected how well the teacher and student communicated and how effectively the student was able to use the teacher's feedback in revising. However, in other research (Conrad & Goldstein, 1999; Goldstein & Kohls, 2002), teacher written commentary, like conference feedback, was not an inherently effective means for giving usable and helpful feedback either. Students did not necessarily revise better and arrive at stronger texts as a result of such feedback. In sum, whether we provide feedback through conferencing or written commentary, the key consideration is what makes feedback *effective*. The chapters that follow are dedicated to delineating just what can be done to improve teacher written feedback so that students can learn to revise, can produce stronger texts, and become stronger writers.

This book will address teacher commentary and student revision from a number of different perspectives. Chapter 1 looks at what constitutes the context within which commentary takes place and how contextual factors may affect teacher commentary and student revision. Chapter 2 delineates ways that teachers can create effective processes of communication between teacher and student so that they can give optimal feedback and students can revise successfully. What makes feedback effective is detailed in Chapter 3, as it looks at issues of what teachers might comment on and how. Methods that enable teachers to reflect on practice are addressed in Chapter 4, which also advocates for and discusses how teachers can carry out small-scale research studies to learn about commentary practices. Chapter 5, working with concepts from the preceding chapters, discusses how teacher educators can work with in-service and pre-service L2 writing teachers to help them develop sound commentary practices. In sum, this volume addresses teacher commentary and student revision from several angles: contextual factors, teacher-student communication, the "what and how" of commentary, teacher reflection, teacher research, and teacher education.

Chapter 1

Understanding the Role of Context in Teacher Commentary and Student Revision Response

Understanding How Institutional and Programmatic Context May Affect Commentary

Many factors play a role in teacher commentary and how students use such commentary in revision, and many texts are created and re-created as students write, teachers respond, and students revise. As the figure on page 10 depicts, teachers and students work within complex contexts as they write, comment, and revise. This context is a unique combination of factors stemming from the institution and the program within which the writing, commenting, and revising takes place, as well as factors that teachers and students bring to the process (Goldstein, 2001).

Unfortunately, institutional and programmatic factors have not been considered to any great extent in discussions about providing effective written commentary. It appears that the process of giving written commentary and revising with this commentary has largely been envisioned as a linear one that involves the teacher and the student only. In such a linear model, the student writes a text, the teacher reads it and provides written commentary, and then the student reads the commentary and writes a new text that includes revisions promoted by the teacher's written commentary. This view of the process fails to consider the contextual forces operating on the teacher and the student alike and assumes that the teacher's commentary and the student's texts are created in a

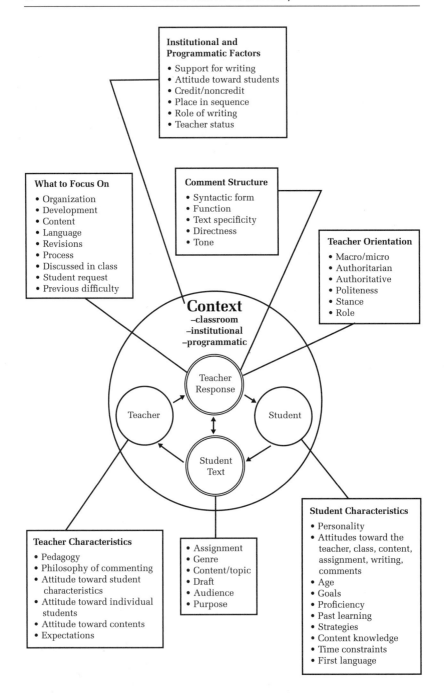

Institutional and Programmatic Factors

• Support for writing
• Attitude toward students
• Credit/noncredit
• Place in sequence
• Role of writing
• Teacher status

What to Focus On

• Organization
• Development
• Content
• Language
• Revisions
• Process
• Discussed in class
• Student request
• Previous difficulty

Comment Structure

• Syntactic form
• Function
• Text specificity
• Directness
• Tone

Teacher Orientation

• Macro/micro
• Authoritarian
• Authoritative
• Politeness
• Stance
• Role

Context
–classroom
–institutional
–programmatic

Teacher Response

Teacher

Student

Student Text

Teacher Characteristics

• Pedagogy
• Philosophy of commenting
• Attitude toward student characteristics
• Attitude toward individual students
• Attitude toward contents
• Expectations

• Assignment
• Genre
• Content/topic
• Draft
• Audience
• Purpose

Student Characteristics

• Personality
• Attitudes toward the teacher, class, content, assignment, writing, comments
• Age
• Goals
• Proficiency
• Past learning
• Strategies
• Content knowledge
• Time constraints
• First language

Fig. 1. The interaction of student, teacher, and context

vacuum. In reality, this is hardly the case: Programmatic and institutional attitudes toward writing, toward writing teachers, and toward different multilingual populations can greatly affect how teachers provide written commentary (see Hyland & Hyland, 2001) and how students react to such commentary and use it in their revisions.

Some teachers and students work within institutions where writing and what someone has to say through writing is highly valued. In such contexts, it is not unusual to see this value transmitted to and through the program where writing is taught. In addition, usually there is support for teachers who believe in responding to the content of their students' work as well as to rhetorical concerns such as purpose, audience, organization, and development. In my experience, teachers and students are well aware of this support. In this context, teachers who share these values may provide commentary marked by attention to content and rhetorical concerns, and such commentary is valued by the students who receive it. I have also seen some teachers who ignore content and rhetoric in favor of sentence-level concerns begin to question their responding practices when they work within such a context, and I have seen some of them make a complete shift.

Conversely, other teachers and students work within contexts where writing, at least for multilingual writers, is seen as an exercise in developing grammatical and lexical expertise. Even teachers who do not believe that writing instruction should have as its raison d'etre the development of linguistic competence may be hard pressed to provide written commentary on content and rhetorical concerns in the manner they believe is effective because of the pressure to respond to students' grammatical and lexical errors first and foremost.

Additionally, some research has shown that students' attitudes are affected by programmatic attitudes and how the teacher responds (Hedgcock & Lefkowitz, 1994, 1996) so that students whose teachers stress accuracy may prefer feedback that focuses on accuracy, and students whose teachers stress content and rhetorical concerns may prefer feedback that focuses on these areas. Clearly students are also affected by the responding practices their teachers employ, practices that cannot help but be influenced by the institutional and programmatic context.

No matter what view of writing an institution or program professes to hold, requirements based on number of words, drafts, or papers, plus entrance and exit exams, exert strong pressure on teacher commentary and student revision. For example, some programs require that students write 10,000 words over the course of the semester and that these be "original words"; that is, they must not be words in a second or subsequent draft of the original text. In such a context, students find it difficult to find time to revise since they need to churn out new texts with original words and are therefore less open to revision since it doesn't "count." Teachers here struggle with not overburdening their students by requiring drafts and revisions and certainly struggle with determining to *what* they should respond as well as *how much* and *how* they should respond. Some programs have exit exams where sentence-level accuracy is accorded the greatest weight. In these situations, students and teachers alike may feel the pressure to concentrate far more than they would choose on such sentence-level concerns in the commentary and revision process (see Cohen & Cavalcanti, 1990).

Sociopolitical forces also need to be considered (Benesch, 2001; Severino, 1998; see also Canagarajah's 2002 volume in this series). In some institutions, where negative attitudes toward minorities exist, multilingual writers are marginalized. Often this translates into large classes, heavy teaching loads for full-time faculty, and an over reliance on adjunct faculty. I once taught in a program where negative attitudes toward minority students, most of whom were Generation 1.5 students, were pervasive. Because the institution would not give us a sufficient number of faculty, we regularly turned away hundreds of students each semester from writing courses they needed and were required to take. In addition, the hundreds of students that actually were in classes were served by five full-time faculty members and many adjunct faculty members. Full-time faculty with four classes of 25–30 students found it very difficult to give as much, as frequent, and as effective commentary as they would have liked. Adjunct faculty, who needed to teach at several institutions in order to make ends meet, also found it difficult to provide written commentary in ways they would have preferred.

In other institutions, positive attitudes and welcoming practices await multilingual writers. In another context where I taught in which such positive attitudes were prevalent, writing classes were predominately staffed by full-time faculty, class size was held to 12, and teachers were regularly paid an extra unit if the class size was over eight to acknowledge the workload of responding to student papers. Not surprisingly, teachers in this program had the needed time and support to respond without compromise.

Providing Commentary within Specific Institutional and Programmatic Constraints

Clearly, the context created by institutional and programmatic constraints must be considered when a teacher makes decisions about how best to provide written commentary. Teachers who work within contexts conducive to sound practices are able to carry on as they might wish. But what about those who find themselves in contexts that militate against sound, effective commentary? There are many positions one can take.

We need to begin by approaching each teaching situation with the full recognition that we do not teach in a vacuum and we need to understand fully the context within which we are working. Teachers can assess the context through observation and informal discussions and interviews of administrators, fellow faculty, and students. For example, if students are matriculated in degree programs, key information should include what types of writing students need to complete for their courses, as well as the expectations of their content professors. It is important to know, for example, how these professors respond to the writing of second language students. In some contexts, second language writers are graded strictly on their control of content, and difficulties with organization, development, or sentence-level errors are ignored. Often in such contexts, students receive high grades on papers where there are serious rhetorical difficulties. Knowing this about the context would allow the L2 writing teacher to have an open discussion with students about the reasons why the writing teacher attends to rhetorical concerns, and not just content, in responding to the students' papers. In my experience, ignoring the disparate ways that content teachers and writing teachers respond often leads to student confusion and dissatisfaction with the writing teacher's responding practices and the requirements of revision.

Regardless of program type, other key information to be discovered includes:

1. What are the attitudes and expectations of the institution toward your students?
2. What are the attitudes and expectations of the program toward your students?
3. If there are conflicts between the institutional and programmatic attitudes, who mediates these conflicts, and how?
4. What are the professed philosophies of the program and its administrators toward what teachers should be commenting and how?
5. What are the range of commenting practices the teachers actually employ?
6. What are the entrance and exit requirements for the program and for individual courses within the program?
7. How do teachers and students mediate between the requirements and sound commenting and revision practices when there are conflicts between these requirements and such practices?
8. What is the workload for the teacher and the student—that is, what is the average class size and what, if any, are the requirements for number of papers, drafts, and revisions and number of words completed per semester?

Once teachers have discovered the answers to these questions, decisions need to be made about how to best work within a given set of contextual factors. Rarely do teachers find themselves in complete harmony with any one set of contextual factors. As a result, teachers need to first decide which factors they can accommodate and how. If, for example, a teacher works within a program where there is an exit exam that is largely assessed on grammatical accuracy, that teacher needs to find a way to give effective commentary on rhetorical concerns while also preparing the students for this exit exam. When confronted with this situation in a program for Generation 1.5 students, my solution was to have my students do two types of writing, in-class exam writing and regular essay writing. I responded differently to each type of writing, and I spent considerable time in the beginning of the semester explaining to my students what we would be doing and why. In particular, I focused on the nature of the written commentary they would receive from me and how and why it would differ on the exams as opposed to their regular writing.

It is also important to identify and differentiate between those contextual factors that are quite open to modification or change and those that are largely impervious to any modification or change. For example, teachers may find themselves working in an IEP where their students are segregated from native speakers of English and the life of the institution as a whole. Some students may be preparing to enter an academic program but have little access to students and faculty in the program for which they are preparing. The teacher and the students can embark together on an investigation of the types of writing students do in these programs and the types of written commentary students receive from their professors. The teacher could then tailor a writing assignment to the students' future areas of study and ask selected faculty members to be co-commentators on the students' writing. This is just one example of how a situation could be modified.

The factors that cannot be readily modified are of course the most troubling. These often revolve around negative institutional and programmatic attitudes toward student populations and the effect such attitudes have on aspects of programs such as class size or the nature of exit requirements. Here we enter the realm of critical pedagogy and what steps, if any, teachers and students are able or willing to take to redress these negative factors (Benesch, 2001). Critical pedagogy asks teachers and students to assess the relationships of power and how the distribution of power affects what happens within the context. As Canagarajah (2002) suggests in his book *Critical Academic Writing and Multilingual Students,* both teachers and students can be negatively affected within contexts where power is unfairly and unevenly distributed. For example, in my own experiences, I have seen that marginalized L2 writing teachers who work as adjuncts and are teaching four or five classes of composition with 30 students in each class may lack the resources of time and energy to provide the extensive commentary they would like. In such a situation, teachers are frustrated and demoralized, and students do not receive as optimal feedback as they might. Canagarajah provides a detailed account of ways that such power imbalances can be contested. However, because every context is different and the consequences for teachers and students of critical action in any one situation cannot be predicted here, I will not make a blanket recommendation that teachers redress all power inequities. That is, like Pennycook (2001), I believe that when enacting critical pedagogy, we need to be careful to "do no harm" and to carefully assess what effects any work to redress power will have on our students.

Years ago, as a beginning teacher of writing at an urban community college, I attempted to change what I felt was the misguided use of institutional power, and I ended up doing more harm than good. Students in my composition class were ill prepared for the rigors of academic writing and, consequently, I found that one semester of instruction in the first-level of courses was insufficient to prepare students for the next level. I felt strongly that the failure was not my students' but the system's in expecting that students could possibly be prepared within one semester to move to the next course. As a result, I successfully lobbied for the creation of an "in progress" (IP) grade instead of a C or D for students who had done all of the work but were not yet ready for the next course. I also convinced the institution to allow for a second semester of the course where students with IP grades could continue to work to gain the proficiencies they needed before progressing to the next level. My students were furious with me and felt that I had betrayed them. They felt the IP grade represented a failure on their part and wanted instead to receive the C or D and move onto the next course level, even if they were not ready to do so. What I failed to do is include them from the very beginning to learn how they felt about their readiness and their grades and what actions we might take together.

Sometimes teachers may find that certain conditions can't be changed, as I did when teaching a class of 32 students in an urban California university where budget constraints at that time would not allow for hiring more faculty. However, while the long-term solution was to lobby for more of the university funds to go to the needs of these Generation 1.5 students, the immediate situation demanded that I figure out how to work best with 32 students in providing effective feedback. In discussions with my students, we made several decisions. We divided the class into two. Each week I gave written feedback to half the class and met individually in conference with students from the other half. In addition, we discussed that it is the writers who actually decide who responds to their writing and how making such decisions was part of being effective writers. This meant, thus, that instead of my demanding that they turn in every draft for my commentary, as the semester progressed, they made the decision as to which drafts to submit for commentary and which drafts they might share with others, such as peers.

What I recommend, therefore, is that teachers and students together identify factors that will affect them, including those that could negatively affect responding practices and revision practices. Teachers and students can look carefully at what they can do to remedy the situation and make an informed decision about what, if anything, they will do to ameliorate these conditions in ways that no harm is done.

Taking Student and Teacher Factors into Account as They Shape Context and Commentary

In addition to institutional and programmatic context, we need to also consider what we bring as teachers to the process and what our students bring. Context can be defined both by institutional factors as discussed in the previous section and as the interaction of these factors with what teachers and students bring to the processes of commentary and revision. The unique interaction between teacher factors and individual factors also affect how a teacher responds and how a student uses the commentary in revision (Chi, 1999; Prior, 1991). Teacher factors can include, but are not limited to

- teacher personality
- the teacher's pedagogical beliefs about how to comment
- attitudes toward specific student characteristics
- attitudes toward each student
- attitudes toward the content about which students are writing
- knowledge of the contents about which students are writing
- expectations of students at a particular level
- expectations of particular students

Student factors include, but are not limited to

- personality
- age
- goals and expectations
- motivations
- proficiency level
- past learning experiences
- preferred learning styles and strategies
- content knowledge and interest
- time constraints
- attitudes toward the teacher, the class, the content, the writing assignment, and the commentary itself

The interaction of these factors and how they affect commentary and revision can be seen in the following two examples. In one instance (Conrad & Goldstein, 1999), a student wrote about his negative attitudes toward working women, a position I found very disturbing. Because I believed that it was not my place to tell him what to believe, I tried not to reveal my strong negative reaction to his content. Instead, I tried to play devil's advocate with him through my written commentary to get him to consider the other point of view, and I responded "gently" by asking questions so as to not take over his authorship. My philosophy about not usurping the student's authorship is what I brought to my feedback. The student brought a strong need to hang onto his beliefs and a great reluctance to reexamine them. He also brought a concern about time, which meant he refused to consider outside sources because given his course load, this was too time consuming. I acquiesced to this refusal. Later, in retrospect, I realized that I could have held onto my belief of not taking over authorship and still have asked him to consult library sources to see the range of views out there and to provide him with evidence for whatever views he chose (see Reid, 1994). In my commentary I could also have revealed to him my personal reactions and let him know that I didn't expect him to adopt them but that my position was one shared by others and that he would need to counter that. The net result is that my pedagogical beliefs about authorship influenced my commentary, and the student's beliefs about what he should have to revise and what sources he should be required to use influenced how he used and did not use my commentary. Each text that was produced—his original and drafts as well as my subsequent commentaries—were all influenced by these factors.

In another example, in an ongoing research project on an online course (Goldstein & Kohls, 2002), we explored an unproductive interaction between a student, Hoshiko, and her teacher. The teacher's attitude toward the student was negative, particularly because the teacher believed that the student was not putting any effort into her work. To some extent the teacher was correct about the student, who professed to me that she reserved her efforts for her final draft since that was the draft on which she would receive a grade. This strategy was borne out of necessity, she believed, because she had so much work in her degree courses that she had to prioritize. The teacher's commentary to this student, unlike commentary to other students, was often replete with repetitions, that is, she repeated comments from previous commentary. The student, whose initial inclination was to sort through commentary and in early drafts only use those comments deemed "easy" to enact, ignored these repeated comments. This exasperated the teacher, and it showed in the tone of her commentary and the fact that she repeated comments verbatim from draft to draft. Because she believed the student to be lazy, the teacher never discussed with the student why the student was ignoring the commentary and whether or not she was having any difficulty. The student, not getting new or useful commentary, nor being asked about why she was ignoring so much of the teacher's commentary, continued to employ her strategies of ignoring certain comments. Here again we see how teacher and student factors affected commentary and revision and interacted with each other as the teacher and student worked at cross-purposes.

How do we take into account these teacher and student factors? Teachers need to begin by taking an inventory of their own factors. Essentially, teachers should work from a perspective of heightened consciousness about what they do and why when they provide written commentary on their students' writing. In other words, teachers should articulate to themselves what their "theory" of commentary is and why. As will be discussed in the chapter on reflective teaching, this articulation should lead to a careful examination of the teacher's commentary, including both the form and the content of this commentary, to decide on what is working and what is not so that any needed changes will be made. In such an examination, teachers should also consider what attitudes the teacher holds toward particular students, particular types of students, particular types of writing, and particular contents and what role(s) these attitudes are playing in how and to what the teacher is responding.

In considering student factors, teachers could conduct needs analyses with their students to uncover student experiences with, preferences for, and attitudes toward written commentary (Ferris & Hedgcock, 1998). Open discussions based on the results of such needs analyses should provide a two-way street where the teacher may modify some of his/her practices to meet the students' needs and the students may modify some of their expectations to better work with how the teacher provides written commentary. Teachers also need to discover how students revise using their commentary and what individual factors work toward or against students revising effectively. Conrad and Goldstein (1999), in their case studies of three L2 writers, show how such factors were key in the decisions these writers made in what they would revise and also how well they revised. One student waited diligently for the teacher to direct her revisions, had great difficulty revising independently, and never alerted the teacher when she did not know what to do in response to teacher commentary; one student was overwhelmed by her time constraints outside the classroom and revised less and less as the semester progressed; and one student felt that support resided within himself rather than also in the experiences of others and in texts and found himself holding onto unchallenged points of view even in the face of teacher commentary that asked him to make revisions.

In another series of case studies, Goldstein and Kohls (2002) found that the three students examined also reacted individually to how they used the teacher's commentary for revision. One student largely ignored the teacher's commentary because of the demands of papers from content courses, while another student had great difficulty revising effectively using the teacher's commentary because she lacked the requisite skills to undertake graduate-level writing. The third student felt that revision was her responsibility and had strong enough skills that she could coordinate and complete assignments for her graduate-level courses and her L2 writing course. She used the teacher's comments critically, that is, she addressed all of the commentary but only used the commentary she felt made sense. This research, along with my personal experiences, strongly suggest to me that teachers need to be acutely aware of the individual factors each student brings that can either work for or against students using teacher commentary effectively. Chapter 2 will detail ways teachers can learn about what students do with teacher commentary and why, so that they best help their students revise effectively.

An Overview of Context

Returning now to Figure 1 (p. 10), we can put all the pieces together to see how factors interact in the creation of multiple texts. Let's look at the example of Hoshiko, extending it to examine the interaction of all the factors that were present as she wrote, as the teacher commented, and as Hoshiko revised. The first text created is the student's (see Figure 1, Student Text). This text is influenced by institutional and programmatic factors as well as all of the student factors mentioned previously, including the student's knowledge of the teacher and her expectations and attitudes. For example, Hoshiko knows that the institution requires her to take the writing course she is presently enrolled in while she simultaneously takes 12 units of required graduate courses. She also knows that her graduate-level professors require papers and that she needs to put time and energy into these papers to get good grades in these required courses. If she doesn't do well in these courses, she will not receive her MA degree. She also realizes that the teacher of her writing course will not grade her paper until the final draft, so she doesn't pay much attention to the drafts that precede the final one or to the teacher's commentary on these drafts, in contrast to her papers in graduate courses, because there are no negative consequences.

This text will also be influenced by experiences with previous texts, including the commentary received on previous texts, and it may also be influenced by texts written in previous classes. She senses that the teacher may have a negative attitude toward her, as the teacher repeats comments and an exasperated tone creeps into her commentary over time. But she has had this teacher before and knows that most likely she will still receive at least a B in the writing course (which is all she needs to stay in good standing) even if she puts in the bare minimum.

The second text (see Figure 1, Teacher Response) is created as the teacher responds to the student's first draft and creates written commentary. This commentary is also influenced by institutional and programmatic factors. The teacher knows that her students are in a bind, carrying 12 units of graduate-level work in addition to her four-unit writing course. She knows from past experience that this is a difficult and sometimes impossible juggling act. While there is work to be done in the writing class, she will not grade her students too harshly. Because she sees writing as a process, she will allow students to draft and will not grade them until the final draft. She is trying, however, to address a small part of the work these students need to do in one of their graduate classes, but there is no programmatic or institutional means for working directly with the graduate-level professor. She needs to respond from what she knows about the students' content and what she knows about the genres they are expected to know.

The process of feedback and revision is also affected by the teacher's factors. The teacher is frustrated by this situation and her status as a part-time instructor. Her frustration is beginning to affect how much time she wants to contribute to building the course. Teacher factors are also mediated by the students' text and the teacher's knowledge of and attitudes toward the students. Hoshiko's text, largely unrevised, contributes to the teacher's frustration. Past and present experiences suggest to her that Hoshiko is lazy; she doesn't look for other explanations for Hoshiko's lack of revision. She also has concerns about Hoshiko's capabilities.

The teacher's text, i.e., the commentary, will have a certain shape. The teacher will have made decisions about the focus of the response (content, purpose, audience, organization, development, or language or some combinations of foci), as well as how to respond in terms of the shape of the comments (e.g., the syntactic form, whether or not to hedge, the use of politeness strategies) and the stance adopted (e.g., authoritarian or authoritative, gatekeeper, interested reader, all-knowing reader). The teacher focuses a lot of her commentary on the form of Hoshiko's writing, concentrating on sentence-level issues and issues such as citation form. She doesn't often push into the harder areas, such as development. The teacher also doesn't really know Hoshiko's content (political science) so doesn't address content issues either. Given her status as a part-time instructor, she doesn't have a relationship with any of the political science professors that would enable her to ask for one of them to also read her student's writing and talk with her about her writing. In commenting, she does not hedge, and she consistently repeats her comments from draft to draft. Working from her impressions of Hoshiko as lazy, she never stops to ask Hoshiko why she is not revising using her commentary. And since Hoshiko does not revise using her commentary, the teacher feels justified in her assessment and in her perceptions.

The student is next influenced by this teacher's text as well as the student factors already in play, some of which may be mediated or changed by the teacher's feedback. Hoshiko continues to place emphasis on her graduate courses, continues to see that she will not be penalized in her writing class for "inadequate" drafts, and continues to be exasperated by her teacher's repeated comments. She never asks her teacher why she repeats her comments, and in fact when she does not know how to revise in response to her teacher's comments, she does not ask. Hoshiko seems to believe that her teacher cannot be questioned. None of these factors are ameliorated. If there are multiple drafts, the student creates a new text, the teacher writes a new commentary text, and so on. All of these texts are also continually influenced by the institutional and programmatic factors discussed previously.

What we have, therefore, is a complex process, with multiple factors interacting and mediating each other, through a cyclical process within which these multiple student texts and teacher commentary texts are created, rather than a one-dimensional and a linear process. The issues and practices to be discussed throughout this book will serve to deconstruct this process as well as be informed by this process in arriving at, ultimately, what needs to be considered in providing effective teacher commentary. It is my hope that with a better understanding of all the factors that affect student writing, teacher commentary, and student revision with commentary, teachers can avoid the situation as described for Hoshiko and her teacher.

Chapter 2

Establishing Effective Communication between Teacher and Student

Avoiding Appropriation: Understanding and Responding within the Student's Rhetorical Context

Second language writing teachers are often cautioned against appropriating their students' texts when they provide feedback (see Leki, 1990). Nonetheless, Reid (1994) suggests that we have been overly zealous in our embracing the notion of appropriation and that *appropriation* is largely a mythical fear of ESL teachers. I agree with Reid's argument that appropriation needs to be contextualized—that is, that behavior that might appear to be appropriation is sometimes not appropriation when understood in the context of a particular class, a particular teacher-student relationship, and a particular moment in time. Nonetheless, like Hyland (2000), I believe that Reid is confusing *intervention* with appropriation and that most who write about appropriation are not suggesting that teachers avoid direct intervention through commentary.

Thus, it is important to differentiate between effective intervention and appropriation.

- Commentary that ignores what a student's purpose is for a particular text and attempts either purposefully or accidentally to shift this purpose is *appropriation*; showing a student where he/she is not achieving her/his purpose(s) is helpful *intervention*.

- Commentary demanding that a student shift a position or a point of view is *appropriation*; commentary that suggests a student read about a different point of view or interview others with a different point of view in order to know the other side is helpful *intervention*.
- Commentary that "corrects" sentences or passages without asking the student about the intended meaning risks changing that meaning and is *appropriation*; commentary that asks a student what he/she wants to say and then helps the student find the language to do so is helpful *intervention*.

My experiences while teaching L2 writing and while working with pre- and in-service teachers on their responding behaviors has been that teachers need mechanisms that enable them to recognize and avoid appropriation (Charles, 1990; Cheong, 1994; Conrad & Goldstein, 1999; Leki, 1990; Mlynarczyk, 1996; Reid, 1994). Therefore, we also need to build in ways of communicating that allow teachers to understand what students are hoping to accomplish with a text and thus avoid appropriation.

One of the major ways that teachers appropriate their students' texts is by reading them without knowing for whom the student is writing the text, for what purpose, or both. Once, while reading a paper written by Linh, I was puzzled by her story about her life experiences with her former husband that had led to her divorce and her life experiences after her divorce. The piece she wrote, a narrative of the events leading to this divorce, was fairly detailed and clear, although there were places where what had happened could have been made clearer through more detail and some reorganization. I could have commented by asking for more details or by pointing out where the organization was not clear. I didn't, however, because I had no idea why she was telling me the story. I did not know her purpose and what she wanted me to know or do after reading her story. When I discussed this with her, she explained that she hadn't really meant to tell her story for the sake of telling her story but that she wanted to use what had happened to her to help others learn from her mistakes and find better ways of dealing with the aftermath of divorce. Once I knew that, my feedback to her was drastically different from what I would have given had I not known. Now, instead of commenting on details and organization that would have led her to continue telling her story for its own sake, resulting in a narrative that would not have accomplished her purpose, I began to focus my comments on helping her see what aspects of her story could be used and how, to show others the lessons she wanted to impart. In the end, she wrote the piece she intended, and she learned how to transform a narrative into an expository piece that accomplished her goal. I could not have helped her do this without knowing what her intentions were.

Of concern, too, is the fact that given her respect for my status and power as "teacher," Linh might have allowed me to subvert her purposes if I had just commented on the narrative as a narrative and suggested the revisions to details and organization. As others have pointed out (Chapin & Terdal, 1990; Chi, 1999; Greenhalgh, 1992; Hyland, 2000), students often accept teachers' appropriating their texts because of their perceptions about the teacher's power and/or knowledge. Fortunately, however, Linh did discuss with me what she wanted to accomplish, which allowed me to help her find a rhetorical strategy to do what she wanted to do.

This example illustrates that when teachers and students communicate with each other about the student's rhetorical context, the teacher can avoid appropriating a student's work. A secondary but equally important effect of knowing students' intentions is that when what a student has written does not achieve the student's intentions, we can use our commentary to not only point this out but to teach the student what to do to achieve what the student intends. Thus, we can provide appropriate commentary that will help the student strengthen the text and learn from the revisions for future texts.

Most students, however, do not come to our classes equipped with an understanding of or vocabulary about concepts such as audience, purpose, or points of view that would allow them to communicate with us about these aspects of text. Thus, even before students can communicate with us, we need to work with them to show them what these concepts are and how they influence decisions we make about text. These discussions, of course, are important for learning about writing in and of itself, but my point here is that students cannot communicate to teachers what their intentions are if they haven't had any instruction in the areas suggested previously.

Teachers need to focus some class time on text analysis (Grabe & Kaplan, 1996) through which students come to see how the author's main points, intended audience, and purposes for the text have shaped the text. Students would benefit from a "live" author, such as the teacher, examining a piece that he/she has written. The author can discuss the roles that the main points, intended audience(s), and purpose(s) played in the decisions about such aspects of the text in terms of what to include and not to include, which rhetorical strategies to use for developing the text; this includes, but is not limited to, the types of support used and why and the organizational strategies to use.

In addition, students can work with short published pieces to examine why they look the way they do. Students can discuss for whom each piece is written, what the audience needs and expectations are, what purposes the author has, and how the features of the text (such as its organization, content, and evidence) meets the audience needs and fulfills the writer's purposes. In the following piece from *Newsweek,* students could discuss how the author's audience might be those who can offer the same tax help as he does or help organize others to do so, and his purpose might be to convince these readers to offer such help. Looking at the text, students might notice the types of evidence the author uses to convince his audience: He provides details that show how what he offers is not difficult to do, and he gives examples of how much poor families have benefited from his services.

Helping the Needy Crack the Tax Code

By Bob Burke
Newsweek

April 26 issue - I was fresh out of college and working as a finance consultant in 1994 when I volunteered for my firm's tutoring-and-mentoring program at Holy Family School on Chicago's impoverished West Side. I coached a fifth- and sixth-grade basketball team, but I felt that there was only so much I could do to truly help my kids. Without money to buy food or clothing or sometimes even to keep the heat on, the families in the neighborhood faced a daily struggle that weighed heavily on the children.

One day I had an idea. I knew the federal government had tax credits to ease the burden on working-poor families, but the process for claiming these credits was simply too complicated for most to get the assistance they had coming. I came up with a plan: I would gather a group of business professionals to offer free tax-preparation services. We'd meet at the school on Saturday mornings and get the word out in the community that we were there to help. That December, I spent my two-week vacation scouring the office for volunteers.

The first Saturday we met was rough. The heat went out at the school, so we moved everyone away from the windows to keep them warm. Despite the cold, an amazing thing happened. When the morning was over, the nearly 30 volunteers who had come out agreed that it was one of the most rewarding experiences they had ever had. I can still recall a co-worker's telling me that she could not believe how courageous the families she met were—one woman was working for about $14,000 a year, sending her kids to a local Catholic school to keep them safe and managing a household without a father.

Volunteers for other worthy organizations use their brawn to paint a school or install new playground equipment; I simply asked mine to sit, paper and pencil in hand, across the table from a family in need. In the process, they learned about those they were helping—what the parents did for a living, how many kids they had.

After about an hour, these volunteers usually had the pleasant task of informing a hardworking, low-income family that they would receive thousands of dollars back from the Internal Revenue Service. All that without a commercial tax-preparation service's taking out a big chunk.

I vividly remember when a single mother of two, who hadn't earned enough in three years to file a return, burst into tears when I told her that the IRS had withheld too much from her paychecks and owed *her*

$10,000. She said she would use the money to fix the leaky roof on her house. Others were equally emotional, making plans to pay overdue bills, buy clothes and school supplies for their children or even move to a safer neighborhood.

Ten years after that first morning in the Holy Family School gym, the little program that started with some coordination around the office has grown tremendously. This year more than 1,600 volunteers helped more than 8,000 families receive a total of about $10 million in tax refunds.

That's not only good for these families. That's good for their neighborhoods' economies. We have even begun offering financial-literacy assistance to encourage families to open bank accounts instead of using expensive currency exchanges to pay bills, cash checks or wire money.

I'd love to see this kind of program take off in other communities. With a little dedication, our model can easily be copied. We provide our volunteers with three hours of training, either in the classroom or online. Then they gather at a central location and are bused to schools, churches and community centers around the city. More often than not, we have a tax expert from one of Chicago's premier accounting firms available to address any truly unusual financial situations.

For the most part, the families we serve don't have terribly complicated tax returns—there are no investment portfolios to consider or business expenses to write off. We help these folks take advantage of breaks like the earned-income tax credit, the child tax credit and the child-care credit. While I am grateful that these breaks exist for the working poor, there is something wrong with a process so difficult that it takes a cadre of financial consultants from the city's top companies to help qualified taxpayers claim their deductions.

It has been estimated that it takes an average American more than 10 hours to complete the 1040 tax form. The 1040A, known as the short form, has more than 80 pages of instructions, double the number of lines that appeared in the standard 1040 back in 1945. So much for progress.

The IRS and Congress need to fix the system so that those who need the most financial assistance can get it. Until the federal government makes it easier for the working poor to help themselves, my volunteers and I will be there.

© 2004 Newsweek, Inc.

In addition, students can examine student texts to find instances where students have not yet fulfilled audience and purpose needs. The previously mentioned text (pages 27–28) by Linh about her divorce follows. Here, we can show students that she has shared what has happened to her through her narrative but has not yet fulfilled her purpose of using what happened to her and how she dealt with it to "teach" others mechanisms for surviving a divorce and its aftermath. (All student texts in the book appear as originally written, including all errors and markings.)

Linh

My Life After A Divorce

Rick and I had known each other since we were in High School. We stayed in touch, dated, and were married when I was 19 years old and Rick was 23 years old. After we got married, I kept going to college and Rick had a job as a sales person. He also loved to work as hard as he could to support his family. However, he had a serious problem that I can never tolerate- his drinking habit.

After our wedding, his drinking became even worse. Though I told him many times that drinking alcohol do not resolve the problem, but instead it would ruin his health, my advice was just a waste. At this time, I suffered from seeing his life deteriorating and from his abuse. Even though I loved him very much, I often times thought of getting a divorce. After two years of suffering, I finally decided to file for a divorce and moved to another city.

For the first two months after my divorce, my emotions seemed to be at peace because I was so busy looking for a part-time job and studying at the same time. Because of my busy schedule I did not have a minute to think of Rick. However, once my life was all settled, I began sliding into months of depression. Dinner time and bed time reminded me so much about him. I suddenly realized that those lonely moments devastated my mind.

Since the settlement of my separation, my life drifted into a routine and sadness. Everyday when I came home from work or school, all I did was cook for myself and study. I did not share my feelings. As a result, the more I kept my chagrin deep inside of me, the more I became depressed and lost my memory rapidly. At times I found myself emotionally confused, I laughed and cried at the same time, but I did not know if I was happy or depressed. Worst of all I could not concentrate in my work and my studies.

After my divorce, I had been the après-love victim for a year. Then one evening as Lynette, my new girlfriend, called on me, I grabbed her emotional rescue. I and she talked about my emotional problem, and we finally discovered that I had been isolated myself. To resolve my problem, she suggested that I should get involved in some social events such as getting to know people from my parish or to play some sport activities to keep myself from being lonely.

After listening to her and taking her advice, my life gradually changed since I began going to swim and attending bible study weekly. These activities indeed helped me to relax my mind and relieve my emotional problem from a broken marriage.

With Lynette's help, I recovered from my loss of love significantly. I got back my memory and succeed at work and in class. I am now enjoying my new independence.

When we show students texts such as this one, we can begin by discussing for whom the students think the text was written and for what purposes. Then we can tell students who the actual audience is and what the actual purposes are and discuss why the text has not yet met these expectations. Finally, we can talk about how the writer could revise her text to make it meet the audience and purpose needs and then share her actual revision.

Linh

Draft Two

With today's American life style, divorce is often thought of as one of the facts of life. While this fact of life brings painful experience to divorced couple, the trauma can be gradually relieved through various activities such as social and charitable activities.

Five years ago when I was one of the parties involved in a divorce case, my life was devastated from the fact of loosing my husband forever. After the settlement of my divorce, my life drifted into a routine and melancholy. Day after day went I work from 9 to 5 and came home to find myself lonely in a quiet studio. I could not find anyone I could confide in. Therefore, the more I kept my chagrin deep inside me, the more I became depressed and lost my memory rapidly. At night I always thought of my ex-husband until I fell asleep and woke up to find myself surrounded with objects, and another sad, lonely day started its cycle again. At times I found myself emotionally confused. I laughed and cried at the same time, but I totally did not know whether I was happy or depressed. Worst of all, I could not concentrate on my work. I could not even remember what I had learned from my job or where I had left off my work, which I had just started working on the day before.

Until one day I learned that my parish had formed a group for divorce people from all ages. I decided to join the group and learned to deal with my problems positively. The group was organized in such a way that every meeting group members would talk about their problems and how they overcame them. These meetings offered me an opportunity to release my emotional tortures and at the same time learn from others' experiences in dealing with this kind of trauma. I also found friends who sympathized with me and comforted me in time of sorrow, and eventually I learned to face with the fact that my marriage was over, and that I ought to gather my emotional strength to rebuild my independent life.

In addition to these meetings, the group also sponsored bake sales, car wash, lottery ticket sales, and holiday dinner parties to raise fund for the parish. Weekly, I participated these fund raising activities, and as a result, my involvement in these programs, my life became more productive in a meaningful way. I was pleased that this lonely, miserable period was replaced by these charitable activities.

It is everyone's desire to have a happy marriage; however, if one's marriage ends in divorce, like anything else, there are ways to restore one's life from the trauma. Social activities such as church activities, sharing with people who have the same experiences, and charitable activities are some of the recommendable ways to relieve the painful emotional experience.

The students can analyze the revision to see the differences between the first and second drafts and to see how the revisions make the text more effective by more appropriately meeting audience and purpose needs. In Linh's example, they can see that she has not just relayed her story but used the details as part of her discussion of how to survive a divorce. In this subsequent draft she has moved to a more detailed discussion of what she did to recover and how what she did helped her, details of which were missing from the previous draft.

Students also need to spend some time in class under the teacher's direction thinking about their work and what decisions they need to make. Full-class discussions about individual student's work and their decisions as well as small-group discussions can help students learn to think critically about their work, what they hope to accomplish, and what rhetorical resources they have available to them to achieve what they want to with a particular text (Grabe & Kaplan, 1996). Teachers can also use these discussions as an opportunity to intervene when students have difficulty either identifying or articulating their intentions and strategies or can also work one-on-one with students as they are working in pairs or small groups.

One goal of such discussions and class practice is to enable students to communicate their intentions to their readers. When we provide written commentary, we are usually somewhere other than the classroom and our students are not present as we are reading their papers and writing our feedback. Therefore, we need to determine what mechanisms we can employ to help students communicate with us when we are not face-to-face, and specifically what students can do to inform us about what they are trying to accomplish. The starting point of this communication needs, of course, to be the student. Students need to let us know their intentions, their audiences, and their points of view so we can read and respond appropriately. Once the teacher and the students feel they are ready, teachers need to create assignments that allow students to let the teachers know their intentions. Students can either complete cover sheets or attach them to their papers when they turn them in or directly annotate their texts, noting on the text who the audience is and what the purposes are.

Cover sheets can indicate to the reader (teacher) who the intended audience is, what points/views the student would like to communicate, and what purposes the student has for the text. These sheets can be varied to fit a variety of writing assignments to meet the needs of students in a variety of contexts and at different proficiency levels. For example, students with a low level of proficiency in an IEP or ELI might be working on a piece that describes an object so that someone not seeing it could guess what it is. A cover sheet might indicate that the audience is someone who has not seen the object and the purpose is to describe the object in such a way that the reader can guess what it is. Such a cover sheet might look like the following:

Cover Sheet for a Descriptive Essay about an Object

- Who is your audience? (Who will read your description?)
- What object are you describing for your audience to guess?
- What is your purpose in writing your description of this object?
- What descriptive words did you use to describe your object?
- How will these words help your readers guess what this object is?
- Do you use any words your audience may not know? If yes, what words could you change them to so your readers will know the words?
- What words do you use that you feel will help your readers guess your object correctly?
- What would you like me to look at and comment on so your description helps your reader guess your object?

In contrast, a Generation 1.5 student in an ESL writing class that is adjuncted to a sociology class and who is working on a piece for the sociology class that will first be read by the writing teacher might indicate that the audience is other than the writing teacher or, in addition to the writing teacher, might indicate what this audience brings to the reading of the text—that is, what this audience already knows and believes. Providing this information not only recognizes its importance to the writing of the student's text but also its importance to the writing teacher who needs this knowledge to read the text in the way that it is intended. In this instance, the writer might also indicate what he/she wishes to achieve (purposes), and here because the paper is intended for a sociology audience, might also indicate why this purpose is a legitimate one for this audience, again important information not only for the writer but also for the writing teacher who may not have this knowledge about appropriate purposes. In addition, in an adjunct writing class, the writer can share the writing assignment and comment on how the paper fulfills the assignment so that the writing teacher can also read with this in mind. This cover sheet might look like this:

Cover Sheet for an Essay Written for a Sociology Class

- Who is your audience?
- What does your audience expect you to do in your paper? (What does the assignment require you to do?)
- In what ways (be specific) does your paper meet the requirements of the assignment?
- What background information does your audience have about your content?
- How does this background information affect what you write about and what terms you do and do not define?
- What attitudes and beliefs does your audience have toward your content?
- How do these attitudes and beliefs affect what you write about and how you write about it?
- What is your purpose?
- How does your purpose fulfill the requirements of the assignment?
- How is this purpose an appropriate one for your audience and assignment?
- What are the strengths of your paper? (Be specific; tell me exactly what and where in the paper you feel the text is effective and why.)
- What are you unsure about and would like feedback on? (Be specific; tell me exactly what and where in the paper you have questions and tell me exactly what your concerns are.)

What these two examples illustrate is that there is no one set format for a cover sheet and that cover sheets need to be adjusted to fit the context, the assignment, the draft, and the needs and level of the students. Teachers need to determine what types of information they need to effectively read their students' papers and then craft cover sheets that will allow students to impart this information. Teachers can also develop the cover sheets with the students for each assignment so that students can use their knowledge critically to determine what they need to be aware of as they write and what they need to convey to their teacher on the cover sheet.

In addition to a cover sheet, students can also annotate their texts to look not only at the text as a whole but also at the component parts and how they serve to achieve their purposes and meet the needs of their audiences. In essence, students can annotate each paragraph, indicating what the paragraph is intended to accomplish in and of itself as well as how the paragraph works within the paper as a whole to achieve the writer's purpose and meet the needs of the audience. Such annotations allow teachers into the writer's thinking and decision-making processes so that they can avoid commentary that would take the student in an unintended direction and can alert the student when the strategies used are not working (and what strategies might work).

In sum, teachers do have a responsibility to intervene with commentary not only to help students make a particular paper more effective but also to allow students to learn from their commentary so they can use what they have learned in subsequent papers. This responsibility, however, entails avoiding reading the student's paper in a rhetorical vacuum. Teachers need to teach students about rhetorical context, how it shapes their text, and how to communicate information about their rhetorical contexts to their teachers. They also need to provide mechanisms for students to communicate such information when they turn in their papers, and they need to read within these contexts when they read their students' work.

Listening to Teachers: Educating Students about Teacher Commentary

Some have depicted teacher commentary as not particularly helpful or confusing (see Leki, 1990, for example) while teachers have decried their students' lack of attention to or infrequent use of teacher commentary (see Goldstein & Kohls, 2002). In examining research, however, it is difficult to draw conclusions about the actual quality of teacher feedback, including whether or not it is helpful, confusing, or actually used by students. First, some who have expressed concern about the ineffectualness of teacher written commentary have based their conclusions on studies that largely focused on sentence-level concerns (e.g., Leki, 1990), and some may be tempted to extrapolate from these findings that all teacher commentary is of dubious help. Others (e.g., Zamel, 1985) have overgeneralized to all L2 teachers the findings from one group of teachers who provided ineffectual commentary.

In fact, there are relatively few studies that focus on L2 writers and teachers to look at what individual students actually do with teacher commentary, and in particular to examine the relationship between teacher commentary and student revision on macro-level issues such as audience, purpose, logic, content, organization, and development. Those that do (see, e.g., Chi, 1999; Conrad & Goldstein, 1999; Goldstein & Kohls, 2002; Hyland, 1998, 2000) have found that students vary in how they use the commentary they receive from their teachers.

Some studies show that students find teachers' written commentary helpful (Anglada, 1995; Cohen, 1991; Crawford, 1992; Hyland, 1998; Saito, 1994), but there is ample evidence that there is variation among students in terms of how helpful they find their teachers' written feedback and how well they understand their teachers' feedback. There is some evidence that students do find some commentary confusing (Arndt, 1993; Chapin & Terdal, 1990; Conrad & Goldstein, 1999; Crawford, 1992; Goldstein & Kohls, 2002) and that even when they do ostensibly understand a comment, students may have difficulty figuring out a strategy for revising (Chapin & Terdal, 1990). Additionally, teachers report that sometimes students think they have understood a comment when they have not or that their comments have been misconstrued (Arndt, 1993; Goldstein & Kohls, 2002). Research has also shown that the students differ in terms of how much they feel they have understood of their teacher's commentary. Anglada (1995) found that seven students felt that they had understood from 76–100 percent of the teacher's commentary while two students said they understood only 57–76 percent. In Cohen & Cavalcanti's (1990) report on three case study participants, the highest-level student reported not understanding 50 percent of the comments or how to deal with them; the intermediate-level student reported not understanding 26 percent of the feedback and not knowing what to do with 37 percent of the feedback; and the lowest-level student reported not understanding 62 percent of the feedback and not knowing how to handle 81 percent of the feedback. Brice (1995) also found variation among her case study subjects, ranging from one student (Victor) who indicated a medium-to-high level of understanding, to another (Michelle) who had more difficulty understanding her teacher's feedback. In Ferris (1995), 50 percent of the students said they never had any difficulty understanding their teachers' feedback, meaning that 50 percent had at least some difficulty. Students also report using teacher written feedback without understanding the reasons behind it (Crawford, 1992; Hyland, 1998, 2000).

Students also vary in terms of how successfully they are able to use the teacher's feedback to revise (Conrad & Goldstein, 1999; Ferris, 1997; Goldstein & Kohls, 2002), and some report understanding the feedback but not knowing how to use it to revise (Conrad & Goldstein, 1999; Goldstein & Kohls, 2002). They also differ in terms of how open they are to revising with teachers' feedback (Conrad & Goldstein, 1999; Enginarlar, 1993; Goldstein & Kohls, 2002; Radecki & Swales, 1988). Some studies show that students range in terms of how much of their teacher's feedback they actually use (Chapin & Terdal, 1990; Cohen, 1991; Conrad & Goldstein, 1999; Ferris, 1997; Goldstein & Kohls, 2002).

These studies respectively involve ESL students in the United States and New Zealand; EFL students in Argentina, Taiwan, Brazil, Hong Kong and Turkey; ESL and EFL students in ELIs at a variety of levels; ESL and EFL students in EAP and ESP courses; ESL, Generation 1.5, and EFL undergraduate students in sheltered pre-freshman composition courses, freshman, and advanced writing courses; and ESL graduate students in political science and engineering. It is clear, therefore, that students in a range of contexts, at a range of proficiency levels, and writing for a range of purposes have difficulties understanding teacher feedback, difficulty knowing what to do with teacher feedback, and degrees of willingness to use teacher feedback.

Since research shows variation among students in their actual or professed ability to understand the teacher's commentary and to enact it, this also suggests that factors in addition to the actual commentary play a role when students interpret and enact feedback. For example, Conrad and Goldstein (1999) found that while some comments were difficult to understand, the students' revisions after feedback were also affected by other factors such as content knowledge, student beliefs, and time constraints. The research suggests, therefore, that teachers and students alike would benefit from open conversations that help students understand how to interpret and use teacher commentary while revising and that allow teachers to understand what practices enable students to effectively use their commentary.

There are a number of possible explanations for the difficulties students profess or actually have. One possibility is the quality of the commentary itself—that the way in which it is written is unclear or not helpful. The next chapter will focus on what factors might affect the quality of teachers' commentary. A second possibility is that there are factors that students bring to the process of reading and working with teacher commentary that may militate against their using the commentary successfully. These will be discussed in the next section of this chapter about students communicating with teachers.

A third possibility, to be addressed here, is that students do not always know how to interpret teachers' feedback (Anglada, 1995; Arndt, 1993; Chapin & Terdal, 1990; Chi, 1999; Conrad & Goldstein, 1999; Crawford, 1992; Ferris, 1995, 1998; Goldstein & Kohls, 2002) and that they do not always have strategies for enacting the feedback they receive (Cohen, 1991; Conrad & Goldstein, 1999; Goldstein & Kohls, 2002). Teachers need, therefore, to educate students about their commentary practices and the rationales behind what they do, they need to educate students how to interpret their comments, and they need to teach students how to revise using their comments.

Students come into our classes never having had any writing instruction in English before, having had no writing instruction in any language, or having had writing instruction from other teachers. Thus, they either have no experience at all with teacher written commentary or may have received past commentary that is quite different from what their current teacher uses. And, even if students receive commentary similar to what they have received before, their previous teachers may not have explained their pedagogical rationales behind how they provide commentary. Teachers should not expect that students will buy into what they do just because they are the teacher. The first step therefore is for teachers to explain to students what they do and why (Arndt, 1993; Chi, 1999; Conrad & Goldstein, 1999; Crawford, 1992; Ferris, 1995; Hyland, 1998, 2000; Reid, 1994) to avoid a mismatch between what the teacher does and what the students expect (Paulus, 1999; Radecki & Swales, 1988). Let's take, for example, a teacher who believes that commenting on sentence-level concerns should wait until late drafts and therefore comments strictly on content and rhetorical concerns in earlier drafts. Perhaps some students have worked in previous classes with teachers who comment on everything, including sentence-level errors, in all drafts, or some students believe that teachers who do not correct every error are abrogating their responsibilities as teachers. Confusion and even mistrust about their current teacher's commenting practices may ensue if the teacher does not discuss what he/she is doing and why. In turn, we can expect that such confusion and mistrust will lead to at least some students not effectively using the teacher's commentary.

Teachers can begin the semester by examining the writing of past students and the commentary they received. Discussions can focus on the nature of the commentary and why the students believe such commentary was used. Where students cannot determine the rationales behind the commentary or arrive at rationales different from those of the teacher, the teacher can intercede and explain why he/she commented as he/she did.

In the following examples, students could look at the text and the teacher's comments to see what the comments look like and discuss what they mean and are asking students to do.

Mei

Crack in Family

Nowadays, I can always see posters of missing children or teenagers. I am sure some of them are runaway children. Why is it more run away children in these days than before? I think that probably it is because they feel unhappy to live with their family, or they feel that their parents don't love them. Why is that so? There probably is a gap between the parents and their children since they do not understand each other fully. In my opinion there are three major causes for the lack of mutual understanding between the generations.

First reason of the lack of mutual understanding between parents and children is that some parents do not try to understand their children because they think they are only responsible to give their children good education and enough food to eat. For example, I know a neighbor whose parents having the concept that they are only responsible to raise their child by giving a place for her to live, food for to eat, clothes for her to wear and school for her to study, and should not expect any more form her parents. Therefore, she seldom talks to her parents and she does not bother to try to understand her parents. In addition her parents do not try to understand her too.

- -

Teacher feedback:
I can't yet "feel" the lack of understanding here between the parents and child. I think this is because the discussion doesn't show any lack of understanding. It just states that they do not try to understand each other. I'd like to know what things these parents and child don't understand about each other and how this is a result of them not trying to understand each other.

In this example, we can focus the students' attention on how the teacher provides text-specific comments and explain why she does this instead of just writing, "You need an example here." We can then focus on how this commentary asks for revision of specific types, that is, for details *(what things these parents and child don't understand about each other)* and for explanation of how one thing causes another thing *(and how this is a result of them not trying to understand each other).*

Teachers can also share with their students brief accounts of research studies and what they indicate about how teachers should comment on students' papers (Radecki & Swales, 1988). All of these discussions can be tailored to fit the level of the student, in terms of the level of the language used and the depth and nature of the discussion, and the actual samples of student papers and commentary.

Even with discussions about the reasons behind the teacher's responding behaviors, the studies cited previously strongly suggest that students do not always understand what a particular comment means or what to do in terms of revision in reaction to a particular comment. Thus, discussion of why teachers comment in the ways that they do should then lead to explicit examinations of actual comments, both in terms of what they mean and in terms of what types of revision(s) the comment suggests, as well as how to enact the revisions as exemplified previously. As will be discussed in more depth in the chapter on teachers as researchers, teachers should prepare for these discussions by first carefully examining their commenting behaviors. This examination should allow teachers to determine whether there are patterns in their comments—that is, it should lead to an examination of the relationships among the grammatical forms of comments, the contents of comments, and the intents of comments. For example, in Conrad and Goldstein (1999), the teacher used *how* and *why* questions to get the students to develop their arguments in more depth. However, these students did not necessarily pick up on the intention behind the use of *how* and *why* to signal that revision was needed and that the type of revision needed was analysis and explanation. Had the teacher carefully looked at her feedback practices, she would have seen this pattern in her feedback and could have explained to her students that when they see *how* and *why* questions, these signal that the writer needs to work on the analysis and explanation of the point being made.

Once teachers have a clear sense of how they comment, and the relationships between comment forms and intents, they can share this information with their students by examining selected papers that contain different types of comments and require different types of revisions. Starting with papers written by past students, the class can examine the comments received on one draft and the revisions made in the next draft in response to such comments. These classes can be structured so that, as the semester unfolds, a particular type of revision can be examined. So, for example, working with low-level students in an IEP writing a story about something that happened to them that made them happy, a teacher might bring in papers that received a comment to the effect that the teacher would like to know more details about something the students wrote had happened to them. The teacher can direct the students to the comment; can ask the students what they think the writers could do in response to the comment; and then the teacher and students can examine the second drafts, some of which successfully responded to the teacher's comments and some of which did not. The discussion could then focus on what made the revisions successful or unsuccessful and how one revises in response to the comment being examined. The students' own writing can then be examined to see what they have done in response to the teacher's commentary throughout the semester, and the teacher can intervene in places where students seem to be having difficulty either understanding a comment or knowing how to revise in response to a comment. Finally, after students have had the opportunity to look at papers written by past students and the comments they received, they can also practice interpreting comments on their own papers as a whole class, in small groups, or individually. Such practice will allow students to see what they understand and will allow teachers to intervene when comments are misunderstood.

Depending on the students' needs, the type of writing they are doing, and their proficiency levels, it would also be possible to have classes where many different types of comments and revisions are examined. Teachers need to use their best judgment in deciding whether to focus on a particular type of revision or several types, what revisions to focus on specifically, and when in the semester to do so.

In sum, a teacher should approach each class with the expectation that the students do not already know the philosophies underlying the way the teacher comments; that the students may have expectations that contradict the ways in which the teacher provides feedback; that even when the teacher believes the intent of his/her comments is clear, it may not be to all students; and that even when the intent is clear, students still may not know how to revise in response to teacher comments. Teachers need to use carefully planned and structured activities throughout the semester to teach students how to interpret and enact their comments.

Listening to Students: Educating Teachers about Student Preferences, Needs, and Difficulties

Communication needs to move not just from the teacher to the student as previously discussed but also from the student to the teacher. In order for teachers to comment as effectively as possible and for students to be open to using their commentary, teachers need to understand and acknowledge student reactions and preferences for feedback (Ferris, 1999). In addition, to help students strengthen their writing and make effective revisions, provide appropriate commentary, and intervene where help is needed, teachers need to understand the reasons behind students' revisions in response to their feedback.

In fact, students have expressed definite preferences for and attitudes toward feedback in terms of the types of feedback they receive and the types of problems on which the feedback is focused. They also report using a variety of strategies for working with their teachers' feedback and a variety of reasons for difficulties using feedback or for not using the feedback at all. Importantly, Hedgcock and Lefkowitz (1994) rightly caution us that we should not assume that groups of students are homogeneous in their preferences for types of feedback or the problem areas on which they would like to receive feedback. We can expect to find differences among students within a program and across students in different contexts in terms of their preferences. For example, students in an online writing center in Argentina were primarily concerned with organization, next with content, and felt both were more important areas than were formal issues (Anglada, 1995), while students in Brazil in an IEP wanted comments on content (Cohen & Cavalcanti, 1990). Students in an advanced undergraduate EFL composition class in Brazil varied in their preferences with six out of thirteen wanting more emphasis on content and vocabulary, five out of thirteen wanting more emphasis on organization, and two out of thirteen wanting more emphasis in mechanics and organization (Cohen, 1991).

Students' preferences for comment types also vary across studies and within studies. In examining types of comments preferred by students in EAP and ESP courses in Hong Kong, Arndt (1993) found that students felt that comments that went beyond just correcting were the most helpful, that they preferred that their teachers write their comments next to the text in question, that they wanted feedback that was honest in a positive way, and that they did not like comments that were a "mandate." In Brice's (1995) case study, one student did not like comments that evaluated her writing. Ferris (1995) found that some students did not always agree with the teachers' comments and that questions about content sometimes confused them. Radecki and Swales (1988) and Enginarlar

(1993) discovered that their subjects could be divided into those who were receptive to teacher feedback (receptors), those that were somewhat resistant (semi-resistors), and those that were resistant (resistors). In Radecki and Swales's study, so-called receptors and semi-resistors preferred content-specific comments as well as substantive comments, but receptors also wanted the teacher to correct all sentence-level errors. Among the semi-resistors, whether or not they wanted errors corrected varied by course level. Resistors preferred either a grade or a grade accompanied by short evaluative adjectives and wanted the most serious errors indicated and corrected by the teacher. Radecki and Swales also found that each group had a differing attitude toward different comment types, that graduate students were the most resistant, and that students in the intensive English language institute were most concerned with sentence-level features. In Hyland and Hyland (2001), some students liked positive commentary while others dismissed positive commentary as mitigation devices.

Students also report a variety of strategies for working with their teachers' feedback. Students in Brazil (Cohen, 1991) said that they would make a mental note of the comments, look for places where they were in doubt, and ask for explanations from the teacher. Since revision was not required, few would actually use the comments to revise their work. They also said they would rarely look at a previously written essay. Radecki and Swales (1988) found that while most students said they would read their teacher's comments, most also said they would look at the grade before the comments. In addition, the students reported re-looking at their work after feedback only once or twice, either immediately after receiving it or before an exam. Receptors were open to revising their papers if asked to do so by their teachers, but semi-resistors and resistors were hostile to the idea of revision. Ferris (1995) found that students showed a greater tendency to read and pay attention to teacher commentary on earlier rather than later drafts. In addition, many students said that on earlier drafts they would use a source other than themselves, such as their teacher, tutor, friends, a grammar book, or a dictionary to aid them in understanding the teacher's feedback. In contrast, more than half of the students would rely on themselves in final drafts or do nothing at all. Conrad and Goldstein (1999) found that one of their case study subjects would use all of the teachers' feedback without question while another would pick and choose what to use depending on the work entailed in revising. In Goldstein and Kohls (2002), one of the case study participants chose not to use teacher feedback she felt was inappropriate or wrong.

The research cited here is just a snapshot of what student preferences might be. As Goldstein (2001) discusses in her critique of the research on teacher commentary, it is difficult to make sense of the research as a whole since many of the studies do not detail the pedagogical context in which the study took place, the types of texts the students were writing, the particular draft on which they received feedback, or even how the teacher actually commented. Thus, when we look at some studies where students preferred a particular type of comment or comments on a particular type of problem or expressed preferences for certain strategies when dealing with teacher commentary, we cannot tell why this would be so—in other words, how these preferences might relate to program types, types of writing, what draft they are writing, or how the teacher actually comments.

My purpose here is not to critique the literature on student preferences per se but to caution readers not to extrapolate from any one study and believe that it can predict exactly what their students' preferences or strategies will be. Instead, what the research tells us is that students do have preferences and strategies and that we need to create the means for uncovering these in our classes. We can do so in a number of ways. First, we can ask students to write autobiographies, detailing their past experiences as writers, including as complete a description as possible of the types of feedback they have received from previous teachers, what they did and did not like about this feedback, and what they did after they received the feedback. If they have saved any of their work that has teacher commentary on it, students can be encouraged to attach this work and point to examples that serve as illustrations for what they have detailed in their autobiographies. We can also devise questionnaires in which we ask students about their preferences. Before students answer the questionnaire, teachers need to have discussions with them, with concrete examples, of areas that could receive feedback, types of feedback that could be used, time when feedback could be given (e.g., after each draft, only on early drafts), and where feedback might be given (e.g., next to the text in question, on a separate piece of paper). Teachers can also discuss strategies for dealing with feedback. Such discussions would then equip students to understand and answer the questionnaire. The following is an example of a questionnaire that could be administered at the beginning of the semester of an EAP writing course as a starting place for discussions about preferences and strategies:

Feedback Preferences (please put a check next to the responses that fit you)

1.   I prefer to receive teacher written commentary

At the beginning of my paper

Directly next to the place in my paper where there is a problem

Directly next to the place in my paper where the text is effective

At the end of my paper

A combination of all of the above

A combination of some of the above (specify which)

2.   I would like to receive feedback on

The problems areas in my paper

What is effective in my paper

Both

It depends (tell me what it depends on)

3.   I would like to tell my teacher what I would like to receive feedback on

Always

It depends (specify what it depends on)

My teacher is the only one who should decide what I should receive feedback on

4.   I would like to receive feedback on the ideas and content of my writing

Always

It depends (specify what it depends on)

Never

5. I would like to receive feedback on the organization and development of my ideas.

Always

It depends (specify what it depends on)

Never

6. I would like to receive feedback on errors (grammar, spelling, vocabulary) on all my drafts.

Always

It depends (specify what it depends on)

Never

Strategies (please put a check next to the responses that fit you)

7. When I get my papers back

I read all of the comments and put the paper away

I only look at the grade

I read all of the comments and start thinking about how to revise my paper

It depends (specify what it depends on)

8. When I don't understand a comment

I ignore the comment

I ask a classmate

I ask my teacher

I guess

It depends (specify what it depends on)

9.   When I don't agree with a comment

I ignore the comment
I revise in response to it anyway
I talk with my teacher
It depends (specify what it depends on)

10.   When I understand the comment but don't know how to revise using the comment

I ignore the comment
I ask a classmate
I ask my teacher
I guess
It depends (specify what it depends on)

The point of autobiographies or student preference question-naires is not that these should dictate what a teacher should do. The discussion of student preferences should be coupled with the discussions suggested in the previous section that let students learn about the teacher's preferences for commenting. Combining the teacher's and students' views allows for open discussions of expectations and explorations of where there is a mismatch between these views. In addition, there may be places where the teacher can accommodate his/her practices so that the student will be receptive to the teacher's feedback. For example, although I have discussed with students my view and the reasons behind it that feedback on sentence-level errors should wait until later drafts, some students have told me with great conviction and concern that they want to receive such feedback on earlier drafts. We have been able to find a middle ground, where either the student or I will select some sentence-level areas that she/he would like feedback on for earlier drafts. In another example, in an EAP class, as we work toward students becoming more autonomous, I have explained to students that this entails reading their work critically and attempting to revise on their own. As a result, after the start of the second half of a class, I have told my students that I would only like to see and comment on their final drafts. Some students have panicked and asked me to please provide feedback on earlier drafts. The middle ground we have found here is that I tell the students that part of being a critical reader of one's work is identifying when one needs help and who can provide this help. Thus, I have told them that I would be happy to read earlier drafts but that I would like them to decide when they need me to do this, and I would like them to have read their texts critically first to identify for me those places in the text where they feel they need help/feedback.

As mentioned previously, research has also shown that students do not always revise successfully when using teacher commentary and that sometimes when revising, students do not use some or all of the commentary they have received. In some cases, when students revise unsuccessfully or do not revise at all in response to certain teacher comments, it is because they do not understand the comment or because they do not understand the intent of the comments. There are, in addition, many other reasons for unsuccessful revision or no revision that have been delineated in the literature including

1. not knowing how to revise in response to a particular comment or problem type (Conrad & Goldstein, 1999; Goldstein & Kohls, 2002)
2. not wanting to critically examine one's point of view (Conrad & Goldstein, 1999)
3. feeling that the teacher's feedback is incorrect (Goldstein & Kohls, 2002)
4. lacking the time to do the revisions (Conrad & Goldstein, 1999; Goldstein & Kohls, 2002; Pratt, 1999)
5. lacking the content knowledge to do the revision (Conrad & Goldstein, 1999)
6. feeling the feedback is not reasonable (Anglada, 1995)

7. lacking the motivation (Pratt, 1999)
8. being resistant to revision (Enginarlar, 1993; Radecki & Swales, 1988)
9. feeling distrustful of the teacher's content knowledge (Pratt, 1999)
10. feeling that the teacher's responding behaviors do not meet the student's needs and desires (Hyland, 1998, 2000).

To provide helpful feedback as well as help students use feedback effectively, teachers need to understand what factors are working for and against students using their commentary effectively, given that there are so many possible reasons why in some instances students either do not revise successfully in response to their teachers' comments or do not use their teachers' comments when revising. In the research that I have conducted on teacher written commentary and student revision, I have held conferences with my students during which they have discussed what they did when they revised after commentary and why. I have also held interviews with another teacher's students during which they told me what they did and did not understand, where they had difficulty with using the teacher's commentary, and why they did and did not use their teacher's commentary.

When my student Zohre (Conrad & Goldstein, 1999) told me that she was overwhelmed by a full load of courses in addition to her composition class, that she was working 15 hours a week, and that she wasn't getting enough sleep, this helped me understand why after having done such an excellent job revising her first paper of the term, she did minimal revisions and did not use some of the commentary in her next paper.

When Gin, in my interviews with her (Goldstein & Kohls, 2002), pointed out that she was citing correctly in her draft and that her teacher was incorrect when she gave her feedback that said she was using citations incorrectly, that helped me understand why she had not used the teacher's commentary. (In fact, Gin was correct, and the teacher was wrong).

In another example, Hyland (2000) details a situation where the teacher and student worked at cross-purposes. Here, the teacher commented that the student should use simpler words because he had a number of incorrect or inappropriate word choices, advice the student was both frustrated by and ignored, since he was deliberately trying out complex lexical items as one of his learning strategies.

Teachers also need to understand how their students use their commentary to avoid mischaracterizing students' intents when they are unsuccessful or "ignore" commentary. Such mischaracterizations can lead to frustration and a less effective working relationship between the teacher and the students. In Goldstein and Kohls (2002), in interviews with the teacher, she characterized one student as "lazy," partly because of past experiences with this student and partly because this student often did not revise in response to the teacher's commentary. My interviews with the student uncovered some instances where she avoided revising until the final draft if the revisions were time consuming—first because she was overwhelmed by a full load of graduate courses and felt her attention needed to be on her content courses, and second, because she knew she would not receive a grade on her compositions until the final draft. The teacher never asked this student why she was not revising and so never discussed with the student how this situation could be improved and what help she might need. In another interview, the student told me she was having enormous difficulties with understanding how to enact revisions in response to a particular set of comments about citations. She decided to ignore these comments and not make the revisions. In response, the teacher not having talked with the student, and thus not knowing why she was not revising, kept repeating her comments verbatim on subsequent drafts. The teacher told me in her interview how frustrated she was that the student was ignoring her feedback and that she was certain that this student knew how to revise for this particular problem. She never discussed this with the student, the student never volunteered her difficulties, and so not only were both frustrated by each other, the student also never learned from the teacher what she needed to know.

As the previous examples illustrate, teachers need to understand how students use their commentary and why. Discussions with students after they have revised a paper is one mechanism teachers can use to learn about their students' decisions and difficulties when using their teacher's feedback. Teachers can hold conferences with students where they discuss the students' revisions, intervene where help is needed, and clarify for students where their feedback has not been understood. Such discussions can also lead to the teacher understanding where his/her feedback might actually be inappropriate, and thus not utilized by the student, or to negotiations where the student feels the feedback is inappropriate when in fact it is not.

In addition to conferences, there are a number of written means through which students can communicate with their teachers about their revisions and the use of the teacher's feedback. Ferris (1999) suggests that students attach cover notes explaining how they used the teacher's feedback and why, that they write about how they addressed the feedback or why they chose not to (Ferris, 1998), or that students attach a revise-and-resubmit letter detailing how they used the teacher's feedback (Ferris, 1997). In addition, students can annotate their drafts, explaining throughout what they revised and why, what comments they found difficult to understand, what comments they could understand but did not know how to use for revision, and what comments they chose to not use and why. Such mechanisms give rise to effective communication between teacher and student, encouraging students to use their teachers' feedback in a thoughtful and critical manner and allowing teachers to understand how their feedback is being used to most effectively aid the student.

Conclusion

The following chart summarizes reasons behind teacher-student communication and the means for accomplishing this communication.

WHAT COMMUNICATED	BY WHOM	HOW	WHY
Student's Rhetorical Context (Audience, Purpose)	Student	• Cover Notes • Annotations	• Helps the teacher avoid appropriation • Helps the student read own writing critically • Helps the teacher make decisions about what to comment on
Student's Commentary Preferences	Student	• Preference Questionnaires • Revision Journal	• Helps the teacher understand and meet students' needs • Enables dialogue about differences between student preferences and teacher practices
Student's Strategies for Using Commentary	Student	• Preference Questionnaires • Cover Note • Conference • Revision Journal	• Helps the teacher understand how students use commentary and intervene where strategies could be more effective
Reasons behind What Commentary Is Used and How It Is Used	Student	• Annotations • Revision Journal • Revise and Resubmit Letter • Cover Note	• Helps the teacher understand how students use commentary • Helps teachers understand what factors affect how students use commentary • Enables students to be critical users of commentary • Helps the teacher intervene where students have difficulty understanding commentary • Helps the teacher intervene where students don't know how to revise in response to commentary

What Audience and Purpose Are and How These Affect Composing and Texts	Teacher	• Class discussion with text analyses of published pieces and student texts	• Teach students about audience and purpose • Teach students about revisions to meet audience and purpose needs • Teach students how to articulate audience and purpose in their cover notes
How Teachers Comment	Teacher	• Class discussions with analyses of student texts and accompanying commentary	• Teach students how to understand and work with teacher's commentary • Teach students the pedagogical philosophy behind the teacher's practices

In sum, this chapter has delineated why communication between teachers and students about teacher commentary and student use of commentary when revising is essential and methods through which such communication can take place.

Chapter 3

Understanding the Nature of Effective Commentary

Helping Students Read Their Writing Critically and Communicate Areas on Which They Would Like Feedback

In addition to knowledge of the writer's rhetorical context, teachers also need to discover what areas of concern students have about a particular text. They need to begin the process of responding to a student's text with pencils down, with any personal agendas put away, and with an attentive ear to listen to what their students say they need help with.

I didn't realize this in my own teaching until I was teaching a pre-freshman composition course at an urban institution in 1986. One of my students, Bingo, submitted a draft of a paper with the following questions attached:

Questions about the 3ʳᵈ essay

In the introduction, I say 7ᵗʰ line that "he earn his living out of this 'remote' profession". Do you know what I mean?

You say that in the introduction I don't need evidence to support my idea. But if Patrick tell lie and I sum up the ideas of what his "lie" is, then I may make the wrong introduction. For example, Patrick told me divorce happen one out of 2 marriage and the figure doesn't match this.

In the bottom part of P. 3, I say that violating law is painful and violating custom is disastrous. Is it more effective if I give some example of how painful and disastrous it is?

In the bottom part of p.4 the effect of discrimination is disrespect by friend, disrespect by family and so on. But I think I didn't make the point of how disastrous it was comparing the violating the law. What do you think?

In page 7. I said that the child had to obey their parent & so on to make the effect of hierarchy. But I found that all society more or less also obey parent, abide to custom. In this case, I think I didn't effectively make the comparison of hierarchy and democratic society. What do you think?

In page 3. I use 'rule' rather than 'custom', but in a sense rule is a written law and custom is just commonly acceptable knowledge about some behavior or activity. So there is a difference between 'rule' and 'custom'. Then can I use 'rule'? If not, which words can I use if I don't want to repeat 'custom' again and again?

In top of page 3, I said that the answer lie in its cultural tradition. Do I need to specific and give some detail? I think that cultural tradition that such a broad meaning that it may not be appropriate to use. If not, which words do I need to use?"

On reading his questions, a light bulb went off. I realized that Bingo's questions served several purposes:

1. It allowed him to get feedback on the areas *where he felt he needed it.* By doing so, it gave him control over his writing and the feedback process. This was motivating to him and allowed for his investment in his writing and the process of writing and revision.
2. It alerted me to the areas with which he was having difficulty, something I would not have known from my reading of the text alone.

3. The questions, accompanied by the revisions he had already made, alerted me to what he could revise on his own and with what he needed help.
4. His questions also alerted me to problematic areas of his text he might not have been aware of because he had not asked questions about them.

By looking carefully at the areas for which students request feedback, the areas they have successfully revised from a previous draft (if it is a second or later draft), and problem areas not revised for which no questions are asked, we can devise a much more sound plan for giving feedback than if we are reading our students' papers with only our ideas of what we feel would strengthen their papers.

As I began to ask my students to tell me what specifically they wanted feedback on, I also realized how difficult a task this was for many of them. At all levels of proficiency and in all types of composition classes, from beginning to advanced, from a general composition class focusing on expository prose to a technical writing class focusing on lab reports and research reports in the sciences, students need to learn what makes particular types of writing effective. In Chapter 2, we explored the need for students to learn about how audience and purpose shape text through text analyses of whatever types of texts they need to write, both because they need to learn about this and because they need to learn how to communicate to their teacher what their purposes and audiences are so the teacher can respond within their rhetorical context.

In addition to audience and purpose, students need to examine patterns of organization and development and how they work to meet the needs of an audience, the author's purposes, and the expectations of particular genres within specific discourse communities. Students can benefit from examining effective texts and those that are less effective, contrasting such texts so they can see what makes a text effective and what hinders its effectiveness. For example, the teacher might take a concept such as "providing sufficient information" and examine this in a number of texts that do and do not have sufficient information given the needs of the audience, the purpose of the writer for the text, or the genre expectations. If students are at a lower level in an ELI, this might entail analyzing texts they are writing about an event that had some particular significance to see if there is enough detail to portray the significance of this event to someone who has never experienced it.

For example, in Thu's paper, which follows, missing details make it difficult for the reader to understand crucial aspects of his story, such as why his parents asked him if he had been drinking and what about the experience made him decide to never lie to his parents again.

Thu

Every time I go to the church, Father always talked to us not to tell lies because "lies is a sin" yet I still hear people tell lies everywhere and I am sure no one in the world have not been lies, but sometimes lies could make someone's feeling calm down when he/she got angry. I think lies is not a sin. Once I had lied to my parents and finally I confessed.

When I was in Jinior high school, my parents forbid me not to smoke and drink. One day my friends asked me to cut the classes, instead of attending classes, I went to one of them's home for drinking. By that time my parent's didn't permit me to drink any kinds of alcohols and smoke ciragets, because they think alcohols and ciragettes are harmful to the health. I came home very late on that day, so they looked at me and asked "where had you been all afternoon, had you been drinking?" I'm afraid my parents got angry and fixed up when I said yes. Therefore I smiled and answered "I had been studied with a friend at his home after school." They felt surprised and stared at me "is that true".

Two days later when I came home from school, my father was waiting for me at the living room with a letter, and asked "What should you explain this letter?"

I knew that was a cutting letter from school when I saw it. After a few seconds

silent, I asked him to forgive what I had done.

From that day on I have never lied to my parents until now.

Students in an intermediate-level composition class focusing on taking a stand on a controversial issue might look at whether or not the texts they examine provide sufficient and appropriate enough information to make their stances apparent and convincing. For example, by examining Lin's paper, which follows, the class could focus on places where more information would strengthen her argument about the need to learn English. They could do so by (1) examining the first example, where there is a gap between the Chinese people being able to understand English and arguing with the American people and the American getting punishment, and (2) the gap in her second example, where we don't know how her mother was able to know that Con Edison would fix the gas leak if she didn't speak English and hadn't spoken with the company. Additionally, they could discuss whether or not Con Ed has Chinese-speaking operators in New York City that would have obviated the need for Lin's mother to speak English had she known, a point that would weaken this example as support for her main point. Finally, they can focus on how none of the examples address people who are "paying a visit in the United States."

Lin

I think people in the United States should know English because it is part of

our daily lives which is essential and necessily. There are many advantages for a

person who knows English while he is living or paying a visit in the United States.

Some of the advantages are protection and saving time.

Protection: If you know English, nobody will take advantages of you. Even

though if you might be tricked by someone you will know how you are going to

complain them in order to defense yourself. For example, one day I went by a street. I was told that two cars has accident. One was American car and one was Chinese car. When that American knew that they are Chinese he thought that they wouldn't understand him so he said to his friend in public, "We could push all the mistakes to them. Then we would have few hundred dollars to spend." Unluckily, these Chinese understood English and argued with them. As a result instead of getting advantages from the Chinese, that American got punishment.

Saving time, if you want to do something without speaking English. There is no way you can do it unless you know English. However, you will do it slowly by waiting people to help you. There was one case where was happened to my mother. One day one of my house's gas pipe was broken. It leaked gas. My mother didn't understand any knowledge about gas. Simultaneously, she learned that Con Edison would fix it but she doesn't speak English. Consequently, she left home and waited for her children to come back. Then we called to Con Edison for help. Now, you can say that speed of doing something is very important when you know the language.

In fact by knowing one's language is very important to human being to survive.

In such discussions two things need to happen:

1. Students should learn what makes a text effective for that feature, and they should learn how to identify what is and is not problematic in their own texts in relation to this feature.
2. Students should critically examine their own texts for the feature being discussed to see how effective their texts are.

This, of course, is important in and of itself, but for our purposes here, the key is not only to help students become critical readers of their own texts but to teach them how to make good use of their reader(s) by communicating what they think they need help with—i.e., the aspects of their texts they find problematic and for which they lack revision strategies.

Concurrent with such text analyses and discussions, teachers can help students develop cover sheets that will accompany their writing when submitting it to their readers(s). In Chapter 2, we discussed cover sheets that alert the reader(s) to the students' rhetorical contexts. Here, cover sheets can be expanded to include the following types of information:

- What I like about my paper/What I think is effective.
- What I feel may not be effective and would like feedback on.

In addressing these questions, students need to be specific and explicit—that is, they need to indicate the *specific places/sections/lines* in their paper, annotating what they feel is either effective or problematic, and why. The following is one example of a cover sheet used in a writing course for graduate students who are writing papers for their graduate courses in political science and who are receiving feedback from writing teachers who are not their political science teachers.

WRITING WORKSHOP COVER SHEET

A. Please attach a copy of your assignment along with this cover sheet to your paper.

B. Please turn in your sources used in your paper, and attach a list of these sources to your paper.

C. Please answer the following:

    1. The audience who will read this paper consists of:

    2. This audience will already know the following so I will not have to define or explain these in my paper:

    3. This audience will not know the following, and I will have to define or explain these in my paper:

4. This audience will expect to learn the following from reading my paper:

5. This audience holds the following opinions/attitudes toward my thesis and my purpose:

6. I want my audience to know/do the following after reading my paper:

7. My paper has the following strengths (point out specific places and describe explicitly):

8. I need feedback/help with the following areas in my paper (point out specific places and describe explicitly what you are uncertain about):

Task A might not be included on a cover sheet for papers that are being written for a writing class, and Task B might not be included on a cover sheet for a paper that is not source based, but the remaining tasks are ones that could be used with any writing class and writing assignment. Tasks C1–6 were examined in Chapter 2, where students communicate to their readers what the rhetorical context is so their readers will read their papers appropriately. Tasks C7 and C8 focus on students' communicating what is and what is not working in their papers.

What differs from class to class will be the types of information students might focus on in their answers and the complexity of the answers. So, for example, students at a low level of proficiency would be expected to focus on less complex text features, fewer text features, and do so in a less complex and detailed manner than those at a higher level of proficiency.

The process of analyzing texts, coupled with students providing cover sheets and annotations to their texts, is one that needs to continue throughout the course of a class. In almost all classes, at least some students will continue to have difficulties identifying what they need feedback on and or providing explicit annotations. Thus, teachers should plan on monitoring the cover sheets, providing feedback on these, and intervening whenever students are having difficulties.

Determining What to Comment On

Certainly one point of departure for what to comment on is what the student has communicated he/she needs help with in annotations or on a cover sheet. In most instances, teachers will notice that there are other areas, in addition to the ones students have indicated, that warrant commentary. Where do we begin? If we consider that people write in order to communicate to readers, then logically we need to address places in a text that do not communicate clearly. On the whole I advocate responding to sentence-level issues at a point in the composing process when the writer has worked through whatever text-level issues he/she needs to address (see Ferris, 2001, for a discussion of when to provide feedback on sentence-level errors). Nonetheless, there are occasions where students have difficulty clearly expressing their meaning at the sentence level. For example, when Pilar was writing a paper on making her own decisions, she wrote the following:

Lots of times I have been thinking if how to be a fully matured person so that it might be helpful to have my own decision, to be right all the time especially there are instincts in our life and suddenly it occurred.

In order for me to understand her text as a whole, I needed to understand this particular sentence, which I could not, and so I asked her to tell me what she meant. Whenever we have difficulty understanding a student's text at the sentence level, we need to indicate this and ask the writer to clarify the meaning for us. It is very important in such cases to avoid assuming that we can decipher the writer's intention and to avoid rewriting the student's text. Instead, we need to ask the student what he/she meant so as to avoid changing this meaning.

Sometimes the difficulty lies not just at the sentence level but at the text level when a student has written a text that exhibits the characteristics of writer-based prose that is clear to the writer but has not been adapted to the needs of readers, and so is unclear to the audience (Flower, 1979). While composing in this manner can be a useful heuristic for writers to get their ideas down on paper, eventually, such prose needs to be revised to become reader-based. When Jin handed in the paper that follows, I could not understand it as it was so heavily writer-based. His words, phrases, and ideas were "saturated" with meaning for him (Flower, 1979) but were unclear for me. Additionally, the connections between sentences within paragraphs and across paragraphs were not clear, and I could not see what the paper meant as a whole. (This paper was written in 1986, and all editing shown were the student's.)

Jin: Draft One
Discrimination of the Public Places
(How to discriminate 'em against the public bathroom walls)

Ours is a optimistic society. If you watch Phil Donahue or read US maga-zine, you know this is true. People persue pragmatistical life style. Of course, Great American idealism has always been based on practicality: they believed in geology before astronomy. It was more useful, much like the invension of micro-wave popcorn. So people here tend to consume energy on problem solv-ing. Indeed in sociological and nationalistic problem. You know there are a lot of problem like this.

I think, by now, Americans has become expert on disgrace. They really know the meaning of (inflicting someone and being inflicted?) (It) can be done in abu-sive verbal form or physical manner. When the aim of infliction is intensionaly
-to differenciate – to make a clear distinction,
pointed toward particular group, that is discrimination. Now majority of people

agree that discrimination is wrong.(? ~~They agree that saying offensive thing is wrong.~~) As optimistic nature of human,~~-~~especially Americans, things get better. Our collective moral has changed past stigma to ~~each~~ ^the^ lessons and ^has^‿displayed the psychoes of Pepsi generation. Heave Ho. Nowadays you no longer see typical abusive language and act‿ ^exhibiting, display, exposure^ in public place at high noon.

However, there is one are that has not been appro‿ched ^a^ yet. I don't know if the hesitation stems from ignorance or embrassment, but I do know that ~~the topic~~ it is the (subject/topic) ‿ ^very^ few discuss openly. Public bathroom wall. Grafiti with various slogan and theme. ~~indicate suggest that~~ It is the place which indicate the existence of last American taboo in glance. (?)

Walls of public restroom has always been a informational venue of the mutual interest: ~~sort~~ they function as ~~sort of~~ classifyed ads, or bulleten board sort of thing. Some of the information contains offering of social intercourse, usually sexual interest for heterosexuals or non-heterosexuals. I believe these ads are still permissive, if not healthy. While others graffiti speaks: political slogan and ploaganda. PARA. However, what's not healthy and is remaining ~~bereabal~~ un-reasonable is those descriptive disgrace ~~on~~ ON ~~toward group of people by of different~~ race, social class, religion and ideology. ~~An the plain foul language~~ In another word, just plain, foul language.

When a paper is so writer-based, it doesn't seem possible to give written feedback the reader needs to understand the paper in order to write comments. To comprehend the paper the reader would need to "read into" a lot of what the writer has written and thus risk misinterpreting the writer's meanings. In fact, I asked Jin to come talk with me first before I wrote any comments. During our discussion I learned that sometimes writer-based prose may serve a function other than getting one's ideas on paper, as it did for Jin. Jin told me that because the topic of discrimination was very painful for him, he wrote his paper as a way to distance himself, to be ironic and sarcastic, and to never actually directly address his point. Thus we discussed how he could write his paper, keep his distance, but make his paper reader-based and accessible. His next draft, while still containing writer-based prose, is more reader-based and more comprehensible. (Again, all changes shown are the student's own.)

Jin: Draft Two
Discrimination of the Public Places
(How to discriminate 'em against the public bathroom walls)

Intro #1 By now I think American have become expert on disgrace. They really know the meaning of inflicting someone and being inflicted and know that it can be done quite easily. When the aim is intentionally pointed towards par-ticular group for, of differentiation, that is discrimination. Today, majority of people agree that discrimination is wrong. Our collective moral has stimulated the public awareness and, nowadays, you no longer see ᵪ abusive language and act exhibiting its glance at public place. However, there is one area that has not ~~yet~~ approached yet. I don't know if the hesitation stem from ignorance or from embrassment or simply stupid and not recognized by psychiatry community. Public bathroom wall....

- main body #1

Walls of public restroom have a sole function as a informational venue of the mutual interest: classifyed ads or bulleten ~~bourd~~ board sort of thing. You'll see graffiti all over the place speaking out of political ~~slogan~~ propaganda, social criticism, or religious slogan. Some of them are offering of social intercourse, usually sexual interests for heterosexuals or non-heterosexuals. I believe these ads are still permissive, if not, healthy. However, what is not ~~healthy~~ neither healthy nor permissive and is remaining unreasonable ~~is~~ are those descriptive disgrace on race, social class, religion and ideology. In another word-foul language. I don't know if they are written for particular people or merely someone who use bathroom a lot. But I do know ~~is that most of people~~ people take constructive criticism but not foul language.

The subject varies from Aids patients to jews to black vs. white. The curious thing is that all the excessive ~~opinion/criticism~~ infliction on religion, politics, or ideology leads to ~~racism~~ racial infliction. Christianity relates to jew. Jesus Crist relate to white (which is interesting association, but is popular). Aids relate to homosexuals (obviously), and so on. [Someone ought to do sociological/para psychological studies on this.] I believe that these came mostly from conviction of superiority and inferiority within social group. It is really childish, un-civilized thing, yet it was/has been always ~~major source for~~ one of the major forces of servival in human nature.

However, there are other notions in which taking this as joke. In fact, I don't think ~~many mo~~ many people are taking this too seriously in real life. Come to think of it, racial jokes are usually the high-light of American comedy on T.V. or theater, and, in fact, people ~~love~~ like them. Of course, only to the certain degree. They are ~~constructing~~ developing very thin line between ~~serious~~ sickness and joke and are very hard to determine and justify (- And this is the point ~~that~~ the racial jokes make people laugh about: the nature of human egoism and self-criticism.)

For me, bathroom is a place to think, to sort out the confusing and oppressive realities of day to day life. It is a place I re-unite with the nature and other biological function of human necessities. But at the public restroom, things won't be as peaceful as the bathroom in my house. It is like battle-field. Without any notice or recognition and for no reason, you'll have to take a chance of wheater being offened, descrinminated against the public bathroom ~~wall~~ space. It's such a pity things. Being scared, you'll be haunted by the words written on the wall, and you'll never sit at ease.

In sum, where a student's meaning is not clear, either at the sentence or text level, is where we need to begin our commentary. Sometimes, we will be able to indicate the lack of clarity through written commentary, but sometimes teachers will find it much more productive and helpful to meet with students to help them clarify their meaning.

In addition to considering what students have asked us to respond to and areas that are not clear, we need to consider, first and foremost, whether or not the student has accomplished what he/she has indicated as the purpose of the paper. Often teachers will discover that the student has not fulfilled the stated purpose. Sometimes teachers will even discover that the text has moved in a direction very different from what the writer has indicated as its purpose. Sam had indicated that his purpose in the following paper, written in 1986, was to argue to other Chinese that China needed to reduce its population, but his paper didn't achieve this purpose. Instead his paper addressed a number of other points, including why large families have been valued, how people have reacted to the one-child policy, and why more westernized Chinese societies such as in Hong King accept lowering the population more easily.

Sam

As China accelerates toward economic development and technological mordernization, she is facing a very serious problem- over population. With an estimate of one point five billion people in China today, it is 21.3% of the world population. The Chinese Government didn't recognized the importance until a decade ago. Under the ruling of Moe, he believed that a country would be able to produce more output by increasing labor force, so he encouraged to expand the population after he took over China. However, as China improves its machinary technology after trading with foreign counties, machines are taking place of human workers. As a result, it leads to the decline of the extended family.

There is an old saying in Chinese- "Hundred sons and thousand grandchildren". It may sound exaggerate but it reflects the traditional Chinese family. There are several reasons why large families exist. First of all, since most Chinese are farmers, they need to have more sons in order to share the work in fields. The more children they have, the more help the fathers could get. Secondly, the survival rate was very low in the past. For example, if a family have ten children, it might wind up with only three or four who could survive into adulthood because of poor medications and nutritions. Furthermore, fathers want their sons to carry on their blood line and family names. Therefore, very often a father could have several daughters but one son. My uncle is an prefect example, he had five daughters so he finally gave up. Besides, in the old days, raising a daughter was considered rasing someone's future wife. More-over they could not perform the same duty as the sons could have.

When the "One child policy" was forced in 1979 in China. Some fathers became so frustrated that they could end up with only one daughter, there were thousands of baby girls were killed by their own father. As time went by, people are now accepting the change and face the reality- a generation growing up without brothers and sisters.

As for Chinese people outside China-Hong Kong. Under the influence of western culture and the problem of housing shortage. They easily adopt the concept of having two children is a standard, even there is no restrictions on how many children they should have. For one thing, they understand raising children cost. The expense of food, clothing, medicare, education discourage parents to have many children. And it is true that they realize there is more than finance they would provide: the time, effort, love and patience that parents offer is tremendous.

Overall, I believe that it is essential the population should be under control at all time regardless which country. For we have to face the future problems such as food and energy shortage eventually. The present population of the world is now forty-nine billions. When year 2000 comes, it would increase up to sixty one billion by estimate. By the end of twenty-first century, the number would be today's double. Reducing population is impossible, but we should at least keep it down, just for our children's sake.

In my feedback to Sam I pointed out the mismatch between what he had told me his purpose was and what he wrote, and I asked him what he wanted to do:

You have indicated that your purpose is to convince other Chinese that overpopulation needs to be controlled. You state this clearly in the conclusion of your paper. Yet in the conclusion you also state that "reducing the population is impossible," so I am not sure whether you feel it can be done or not. Some of the paragraphs preceding your conclusion suggest that you don't believe mainland China can reduce its population: You explain the historical reasons that people had large families and seem to suggest that some people still hold to these beliefs. Furthermore, you show the negative effects of the attempt to control overpopulation through the one-child policy when you discuss the killing of baby girls.

Consider what you want to do: If your purpose is to convince other mainland Chinese to control overpopulation, how can you convince them? You need to write arguments that would make them not want to hold onto the desire to have large families. If you want them to control overpopulation through positive means, you need to make arguments that would stop them from killing baby girls. How can you use what you wrote about Hong Kong to convince mainland Chinese that they should share these views?

In contrast, if it is not your purpose to convince mainland Chinese to control population, think about what your purpose is. Your paper as it is written right now suggests that you might want to write about why it is so difficult for mainland Chinese to accept controlling overpopulation, something that a non-Chinese reader would be interested in knowing about and could learn from. If this is your purpose and audience, think about what you can keep in your paper, and what needs to be revised because it doesn't fit this purpose.

In sum, Sam, you decide what direction you want to go in; just make sure in your next draft that whatever purpose and audience you are targeting, your paper fits that purpose and audience.

In cases such as this one where there is an obvious mismatch between the stated purpose and the text, teachers need to point out this mismatch to the student but, most important, teachers need to ask students about their true intentions. I have found that using *if/then* statements such as the ones I used in the example with Sam lets students know what I see as the possible purposes and what the student can do to revise, depending on which of the purposes the student wishes to achieve. My experience has taught me never to assume when there is such a mismatch that what a student has written on a cover sheet should take precedence over the actual text. Teachers need to point out that the purpose stated on the cover sheet is different from the purpose conveyed by the text and show the writer exactly where and why this is so. When I have done so, on numerous occasions, the student has told me that he/she has miscommunicated on the cover sheet as to intended purpose. As a result, instead of revising the draft, the student has subsequently reworded what the intentions are on the cover sheet so that the purpose as stated on the cover sheet now fits with the purpose as conveyed in the text.

Yet, there are instances where the mismatch does result from the text not fulfilling the writer's purpose. Once we know that the mismatch between the cover sheet and the text is a result of this, our task is to figure out why the text does not fulfill the writer's intended purpose(s). What this means is that there are no hard and fast rules about what to comment on in any one draft—no algorithm that suggests responding to main ideas first and coherence second, organization third, development fourth and so on. Teachers need to determine what exactly is not working in the text in a way that the purpose is not being fulfilled. Thus, each response to each student begins not with an "ideal" text superimposed over the writer's text but with where the writer is, what the writer intends, and what the writer needs from the reader in terms of feedback to meet these intentions. One student may have places where the student writes something that is contradictory to what the student intended, and this writer will need to have this pointed out, as did Sam. Another student may provide an argument lacking in sufficient support, which results in a text that is unconvincing and thus needs to have this indicated. Or a different writer may have organized in a way that the intent of an argument is unclear and needs questions that ask about the relationship among sections of the paper and why they are ordered the way they are in light of the writer's purpose.

Let's look at some instructive examples, one focusing on the appropriateness and quality of support for an argument, one where we need more information to understand the importance of the writer's story for him, and one where the paper seems to lack an overall coherence.

Masaki was writing a paper for students who were accepted to his university to study business to convince them that they should study marketing. The main aspect of his paper that stood out for me was his development. In particular, I felt that a prospective student would not be convinced that his school and major were the ones the student should enroll in. Some of the reasons he gave to his audience were not particularly convincing, such as the school being ranked 32nd in the United States; additionally, he did not mention reasons that would be of strong interest, such as the quality of the teaching, the strengths of the curriculum, the help with job placements, or the potential for jobs after graduation. Some of the information in his paper did not seem to be particularly relevant either, such as how marketing works.

Masaki

Dear new student;

Welcome to San Francisco State University Business School. Now, you have an opportunity to choose your major for your career. Through its three departments that provide limited specialization in representative areas of business. The school of business is made up of accounting and finance; business information and computing systems; management and marketing.

SFSU Business School has a definitely good reputation in the field of business world. For instance, it is ranked 4th in California and 32nd in the U.S., according to Baron's college ranking. Therefore, we believe you made a good choice to come here.

Until the end of 2nd year, you must decide your major department and concentration. Here we would like to introduce you some information about marketing concentration which belongs to Department of Management and Marketing.

Definition of marketing is that development and efficient distribution of goods, services, ideas, issues and concepts for chosen consumer segments. In other words, marketing is an exchange process which relates to profitability from the companies to the chosen consumers.

Probably answering the following questions will motivate you to be in this field. Why marketing is more important than the other field of business? Because marketing emphasis study of people and their behavior. Any kind of business deal with people. Nowadays, market has been shifted to a buyer's market- one with an abundance of goods and services. Under these conditions, we must know customers' behavior as well as what they want and need. In order to do so, you sometime depend on statistical data, sometime depend on your intuition.

Marketing is interesting.

My commentary to Masaki addresses the issue of support.

Masaki, think about your purpose and audience, that is, what would convince students that enrolling in the marketing program at your university is the right choice for them? Here are some things I noticed: Most students would want a school that had a higher ranking than 32nd in the United States so this is not a particularly convincing piece of information. Since most of your audience lives in California, you could avoid this problem by just stating that the school is ranked 4th in California (4th is far more convincing than 32nd). Look throughout your paper and make sure that the details you give are truly convincing.

Now, consider what would convince students to attend your school and take up marketing there. Some things to consider are the quality of the teachers, the variety of the classes offered, and the job opportunities after graduation, for example. I would recommend interviewing some students to find out what criteria they used to decide to come to this school -- this would give you ideas of what would convince your audience. Finally, you ask a very important question on page 2, "Why is marketing more important than other studies of business?" In your paper, you tell us what marketing does. That's the place to start, but now go further: What's interesting, exciting, satisfying about studying people and their behavior and then marketing products to them based on what you find out? It's that information that will convince your readers that marketing is a desirable field of study. Consider also what types of jobs people can get, what the job opportunities are, and what the salaries are like -- positive information about these would also be convincing.

In contrast to a case where a student needs to provide more appropriate support, the writer of the following paper needs to provide more details that would help us understand why this was a shameful experience, and why, because he was Korean, he felt he couldn't share this story with his Japanese friends.

This is a very shameful experience to me.

When I visited to Korea first time in 1980.

I took a taxi from airport. It was rainy night and really hard to caught the taxis. Because there are so many people at the airport.

At last, I caught the taxi after I waited about 40 minutes. Then the taxi was begin to run.

After drove about 5 minutes the driver went to other way that was made me feel some fear.

I asked him "why you going this way?"

He said "Oh, don't worry this is a short cut!!"

After a little while he made stop a car and he said "I think there is some trouble with engine."

I was really scared because it was really dark and became terrible rain. He said "I'm sorry but I need your help. Whoud you push my car?"

Then I did. I was of course leave all of my stuff in the car. At the time, I suspected what I going to happen from now.

I added all my power and push the car.

Then he has gone. Yes, he steal my all stuffs. And I never find my stuff again.

I was really sad , but I couldn't tell any my Japanese friends. Because I am Korean.

Source: *From Learning About Language Assessment: Dilemmas, Decisions, and Directions,* 1st edition, by Bailey. © 1998. Reprinted with permission of Heinle, a division of Thomson Learning www.thomsonlearning.com.

The commentary addresses the need to provide details that would help us understand the story better:

I am sorry to hear about what happened to you, and how the taxi driver stole all of your things. This must have been a frightening and upsetting experience for you. I always feel nervous when a taxi driver goes in the wrong direction. I'd like to understand your story better so I have some questions that you can use to add some information to your story. Why was this a shameful experience for you? Why is it that because you are Korean you couldn't tell your Japanese friends what happened? Answering these questions will help the reader understand what the story means to you.

Sometimes we may read a paper where one part does not seem to fit with the rest of it. In a paper about the causes of discrimination, Bingo included the following paragraph:

Then I have heard about the famous book called the "Communist Manifesto" by Karl Marx. In this book, the society is divided into two classes, namely the proletariat and the bourgeoisie. The bourgeoisie are the middle-class who discriminated against the proletariat and exploited them, resulting in never-ending class struggle. The book had influenced Lenin in revolutionizing the world, from which the communist countries were created. From then on, the world is soaked

in the conflict between the communist and the capitalist countries.

In my feedback to him I pointed this out:

- -

I understand your purpose to be to argue for what you see as the causes of discrimination. When I read the paragraph about the *Communist Manifesto*, I don't see yet how the conflicts you describe between classes and between communist and capitalist countries are related to discrimination. You do write that the bourgeoisie discriminate against the proletariat. However, all the other details in the paragraph aren't connected to discrimination.

Read the paragraph again and ask yourself whether you see a connection between explaining the causes of discrimination and the conflicts you describe. If yes, rewrite the paragraph explaining what causes discrimination in these conflicts or how these conflicts result in discrimination. However, if you don't see any connection, then I would take this paragraph out of your paper, as it doesn't fit your purpose.

In considering what to respond to, the essay about having luggage stolen by the cabdriver points to the need to also respond to the student's content. It is easy to forget when we read student writing that writers expect readers to read their texts for the meanings they wish to convey. As teachers we are often busy thinking about what will improve the text, and what the writer needs to learn. We need to be careful, however, not to lose sight of the fact that we are teachers *and* readers. In responding to the writer of the story about stolen luggage, I would want him to know that I was reading his story for what he had to tell me, and not just for how I could help him write it more effectively. Thus, I would want to express my concern for what happened to him. We can respond sympathetically to what a writer has to say as I did, empathetically when we share an experience or emotion, with agreement when we share points of views, with alternative ways of seeing things when we don't, with emotion, with thanks for teaching us something we didn't know, with gratefulness for opening our eyes to something we hadn't considered—that is, with the range of emotions, thoughts, and reactions that we have under normal conditions when we are reading something that someone other than our students has written.

In addition, students also need to learn from our commentary what is effective in their writing. Praise is important for its effective goals—that is, the acknowledgment of the writer and his/her strengths as well as the strengths of the text (Dessner, 1991) and for its strong motivating force (Ferris & Hedgcock, 1998; Lipp, 1995). Praise also serves to reinforce for writers their own perceptions of what is working, helping them to build confidence in the choices they make as they compose and revise. Teachers need to be careful, however, to avoid gratuitous praise and instead to give praise only where it is genuinely deserved (Hyland & Hyland, 2001).

Through commentary that praises, teachers can also educate their students about what is effective in their drafts. Students may have revised something successfully that was previously problematic, they may be attempting something in a draft for the first time, or they may have written a paper that does not have problems typical of previous papers. Learning that what they have done is effective and why teaches them to use similar rhetorical strategies in future papers, and it is empowering.

When Mei wrote a paper about honesty not always being the best policy, I commented on her introduction that *it captured my interest and made me really think about your question about honesty because I could relate to the example and see that honesty might not be the best policy where someone's feelings might get hurt.*

In another of her papers, I commented on her revisions that the change she had made, turning her focus from solely on writing about her English teacher to contrasting her math and English teachers was effective, letting her know that *I find your technique of comparing a teacher without the quality to a teacher with the quality to be an effective one. We can really see why this quality is important in a teacher.*

Commenting on Writing Processes

In addition to responding to students' texts, teachers need to also give feedback on and help with student writing processes. When we read a text, the *product*, we cannot be sure how that product came to be. Without knowing the underlying reasons for the choices our students make when they write, we may miss opportunities for helpful feedback, and we may even give inappropriate and unhelpful feedback. For example, when Tranh (see Conrad & Goldstein, 1999) wrote a paper about discrimination, he included claims that were unsubstantiated or that were supported with inappropriate evidence. Reading his paper, I had no way of knowing why he was having difficulty with support for his claims. The text could not tell me if he didn't understand how to support claims or if he didn't know how to determine if his claims were appropriately supported. In fact, I discovered that neither of these were the case. Instead, the process by which he gathered support caused the problems in his text. Tranh told me that in order to gather evidence for his papers he would ask his friends what they thought, he would usually ask only one of them, and he would usually ask someone who already agreed with him. He wasn't unaware that this was problematic, but he hadn't gone further to consider what other sources were available to him. Knowing this allowed me to work with Tranh on what he needed to know—that is, to explain what the available resources were for finding appropriate evidence. Had I just responded to Tranh's text and not the process used to create the text, I would have commented that his support was inappropriate and why, and thus I would not have helped him to find more effective processes for gathering and using evidence.

Another informative example comes from my research and work with a student named Takara, who had pervasive problems with plagiarism. While her teacher ignored the many instances of plagiarism in her paper, in my discussions with her I discovered that she fully understood what plagiarism was and that she knew that her papers were filled with instances of plagiarism. If she had been my student and I had responded just to the text, I would have pointed out where she had plagiarized, explained why plagiarism was wrong, and asked her to revise to eliminate all plagiarized material. Instead, because I asked *why* she was plagiarizing, I discovered that plagiarism was a strategy she used to compensate for poor reading skills. Because she was unable to understand the sources she was reading and that she needed to cite from in her papers, she resorted to plagiarizing these sources. What I learned, therefore, is that she needed help with reading and not with understanding plagiarizing (Goldstein & Kohls, 2002).

How does a teacher go about discovering what students do as they compose? Researchers often use think-aloud protocols to discover what writers are doing before and during writing. Think-aloud protocols, however, usually are not practical given the time involved for both the teacher and writer. Instead, teachers can discuss process with students, focusing on aspects of process such as what writers do when they plan, generate text, revise text, and evaluate text, and what heuristics are available for accomplishing these processes (see Flower & Hayes, 1981). These discussions lay the groundwork for students articulating to us (or other readers) how they went about composing their texts and what, if any, difficulties they encountered. The student in the example about plagiarism would then have had the means through which she could have told her teacher she was having difficulty understanding what she was reading, and that she understood what plagiarism was but couldn't use the sources in her writing without plagiarizing because she didn't understand them.

Teachers need to also carefully consider what might account for the shape of a student's text and ask questions to confirm their guesses. These questions might take written form on the student's paper. In the example of Takara, in one instance her teacher wrote, *Are these your words or the words of someone else? In order to avoid plagiarism, you should use quotes or paraphrase. When doing so, be sure to include reporting phrases such as: According to the author, this source is a must read for those who consider....* In another instance, her teacher wrote, *This doesn't sound like your words. Please go back and double-check that you are not taking the author's words exactly. Be sure to paraphrase!* Instead, the teacher could have written, *I noticed that in a number of places you have used the exact words of the author you are citing. Can you tell me why you used the exact words? Is there anything I can help you with?* Alternatively, teachers can meet one-on-one to talk about student processes.

Finally, teacher commentary also needs to focus on students' revisions. We need to conceptualize teacher commentary as both looking forward and looking backward. The forward push of commentary provides impetus and help for moving a draft to its next stage. The backward look of commentary allows teachers to see how well students are able to work with their commentary as well as what students have been able to revise on their own. We need to be careful, however, to avoid conceptualizing or practicing looking back as a means for checking to see if students have followed all of our suggestions. In other words, the intent of looking retrospectively at our students' previous drafts is not to see if students have followed every bit of the teacher's advice on the previous draft. Instead, comparing the previous draft to the current draft enables teachers to learn what their students are having difficulty revising as well as how successfully they are revising with the teacher commentary. In addition, it allows teachers to see what students are able to revise on their own in areas for which they have not received commentary. Most important, this shuttling back and forth between the current and previous draft needs to be informed by what students have shared with us through discussion, cover sheets, or annotations (see discussion in Chapter 2) detailing the reasons for their revisions and for using our commentary or not. In sum, teachers can include feedback about the student's revisions: How these revisions are working, alternatives for how the student might revise in places where the revisions are not effective, positive or negative reactions to where the student has or has not agreed with the teacher's feedback, and praise or advice on revisions that the student has attempted on his/her own.

My colleague Robert Kohls asked his students to annotate their revisions. In the following example, one of his students explains what he did in response to Robert's comments:

In your feedback you want me to determine "where the 'holes' and 'gaps' are in other researchers' theories..." But I totally agree with Best Practices and I don't think that there are anybody who thinks that Internet is "useless". But you can ask "So, why do you react?" I react because I strongly believe that Internet is very important for the improvement of Supply Chain Systems and I just want to declare my opinion to my readers.

Robert responded to the student's draft as well as to what he wrote about why he made the revisions that he did.

- -

Hi Melik

Thank you for the revisions on your reaction paper and for your comments. They really helped me understand your perspective. You make a good point about wanting to voice your opinion in favor of the Internet. No one can argue with that. But that's actually the problem. Most well-informed, educated people would probably agree with you. So, in a sense, you're not telling us anything we don't already know. In short, there's a greater sense of purpose that's missing from your paper.

We know from your conclusion that you believe that Supply Chain Management practitioners should not ignore the enormous effect of the Internet. My question is: have they been ignoring it? If they haven't been ignoring it -- and actually make great use of it, then what's the purpose of your argument? Here again, you're telling them something they already know, and informing us what they currently do. Your reaction paper is essentially informative rather than argumentative. If you agree that the Internet is the best way to communicate -- and supply chain management is making use of it, then you need **to argue another reason why they should continue to use it.** I'm not saying that you should change your position, but you need to approach it from a different angle. In other words, give us an additional reason(s) to believe the way we do -- reasons that reinforce what we or supply chain management already believe. Does that make sense? What I see you doing is agreeing with Best Practices, and then changing the focus of your paper by asking which way is the best way. If Best Practices isn't the best source to respond to, then you might reconsider a source that has the best source to react to.

Also, make sure you explain **why** you agree with Best Practices, and why the Internet, for example, is a communication mechanism that should be embraced by supply chain management over the older communication links. **All of these ideas need to be stated in the thesis.** As I said before, we need to know from the beginning **where you stand on this issue, why, and the purpose of why you're writing on this topic.** You don't want to waste your time arguing for the sake of arguing, but to argue with a purpose.

Use of support

When I read your two examples (e.g., Winner (1999) and the bit about older communication), it seemed that instead of arguing in support of a point, you're actually just informing us about facts. Surveying the landscape, as it were.

In closing, I want to let you know that I do like what you wrote, but I want to give you better ways to express what you believe. You've got great potential as an academic writer and I want to make sure that you get the best possible feedback on your writing.

What I would like you to do is to make the necessary revisions on this draft and then resubmit. If you have any questions, please feel free to contact me as soon as possible.

Bob

In sum, the plan for *what* we respond to

- will consider the product and the type of feedback that would help the writer achieve his/her purposes for the text
- will consider the content of the text and what the writer is communicating
- will consider what might help the student if his/her processes are not effective
- on second and subsequent drafts will consider the process of revision including what has or has not been revised and how successfully the writer has revised.

One caveat is in order, however: *In making a plan for what to respond to, teachers should also consider how much they should respond to.* We need to think about how many areas each student can process and work with, and we need to set priorities accordingly. The primary factors we might use in deciding how much to respond to include the proficiency level of the student and what would be realistic, the nature and complexity of the types of revisions needed, and the draft the student is working on (first, second, third, etc.) as well as how these factors interact with each other. For example, in responding to Sam and his paper about overpopulation in China, I focused my commentary solely on what his purpose was and how to fulfill it. Clearly, on reading his text (pages 74–76), we can see problems with organization (the ordering of paragraphs relative to each other, transitions between paragraphs, and coherence within paragraphs). Nonetheless, the prevailing and most important difficulty in his text was one of purpose, and in order to help him concentrate on working through this issue, I prioritized, in order to avoid overwhelming him with too much to deal with at one time. In addition, to comment on all concerns would be treating the paper as a final draft over which I have placed a template of a "perfect" paper, rather than as a paper "in progress." Finally, the other concerns may in fact not be present once Sam revises.

Shaping Teacher Commentary

In addition to considering what we should respond to, we also need to think about *how* we should respond. We might ask whether commentary should be phrased in the form of questions (*Why do you believe telling a white lie is okay?*), statements (*I'd like to know exactly what was written on the bathroom walls.*), or imperatives (*Decide what you want to write about—why controlling overpopulation is important or how to control population, and eliminate text that doesn't fit whatever you choose.*). We might ask whether we should be *explicit* and tell students exactly what to do or whether we should be *implicit*, suggesting what needs to be revised but not how. Should commentary be generic, or general, or should it be text-specific? Additionally, we need to think about where commentary should be placed—for example, should we write comments in the margins next to what is being commented on, at the beginning of a student's paper, in an endnote, or in some combination of these?

Research cannot inform decisions about where to place comments as to date there is no research that has addressed the comparative effectiveness of end, marginal, or initial commentary. My own experience has shown that one strength of marginal or interlinear commentary is that there is no doubt as to what each comment applies; my sense is also that it is physically easier to connect the comment and the text to which the comment applies when they are next to each other. In addition, Ferris and Hedgcock (1998) suggest that marginal commentary has immediacy, as it appears right next to the place where the revision is needed.

As an example, Jan wrote, "For example, women are denied political power as part in decision making, and control over economic resources. For example, women did not vote in national elections until 1920. The Congress is primarily a man's world. By 1980 only five women had been elected to the Senate since 1920. At the beginning of the 1980s there were sixteen Congresswomen and one woman senator versus 429 Congressmen and 99 men senators." In response, Barbara, one of my graduate students, wrote next to Jan's text, *This example is outdated. You need to explain how discrimination happens now because you have told the reader (in ¶ 1) that discrimination still exists.* Here we can see that Barbara's comment refers to a specific place in Jan's text and that by placing the comment right next to that place, Jan can see exactly to what Barbara is referring.

On the other hand, a major strength of end commentary is the ability to be summative, or cumulative, thereby bringing together all of the comments in a way that educates the writer for revision of the paper as well as for future revision. Alternatively, summative and educational comments can be placed initially. In my response to Chu Hua, who wrote a letter to her friend Susan to convince her to visit her hometown of Shanghai, I used summative comments, pointing out specific places in the text and summarizing the comments as a whole:

- -

Chu Hua,
    Shanghai certainly sounds as though there is a lot to do and see there.
    While reading your letter I tried to put myself in Susan's shoes. Thus when reading your section about the historical significance of Shanghai, I wondered what about this would be important to or interesting to Susan. Is she interested in Chinese history? If yes, this is a sound reason for including this discussion. If not, consider whether this would be a convincing reason for her to visit Shanghai and why or whether you should eliminate this section from your paper.
    After reading pages 3-6, I closed my eyes and tried to "see" Shanghai. I learned a lot of things I can do there, but I can do a lot of these things in other cities, too. What is unique about Shanghai that Susan would not be able to find or do elsewhere? This is what you need to discuss to get Susan to want to visit there.
    In summary, as you write your letter to Susan consider your audience (Susan) and your purpose (to convince her to visit Shanghai): Read and ask yourself, what in my paper would convince her—these parts you should keep in. What in my paper isn't convincing—these need to be revised to be convincing or be removed if there is no way to make them convincing. What else could I write about that would make Susan want to visit Shanghai—these discussions need to be added to your paper.

In my own practice, I use a combination of marginal and end commentary. I work from the belief that students need to know exactly where textual problems and textual strengths lie and that they also need summative commentary from which they can extrapolate and learn not just for the current draft but for future writing. I envision commentary as a wonderful recurrent opportunity through which I can individualize instruction.

Despite my own preferences, it is key that teachers decide where exactly to place comments in a way that students can effectively revise using these comments and so that students can learn from these comments for future papers. This decision should be based on the teacher's knowledge of each student's needs and preferences, the nature of the text, and the nature of what is working and what needs revision within the text.

We also need to make decisions about what form our comments will take. Common consensus is that commentary should be text-specific (see Ferris & Hedgcock, 1998). While Ferris (1997) cautions that it is not completely clear-cut what is and what is not a text-specific comment, there is agreement that text-specific commentary is commentary that could only apply to that writer's text at that place in the text. Text-specific comments serve to show exactly what difficulties the reader is having with the text and where, and they are also motivating because they show the reader actively engaging with the writer's text.

The following response is text-specific—that is, the comment can only apply to this student's text and no other text.

Student's Text:

The first reason for discrimination is ignorance. The dominant group ignores some characteristics of the minority selecting out those traits that are defined as significant and identifying people as "subordinate" on the basis of them. The dominate group does not realize that a white and black person are made of the same substance. They both eat. They both breath. This group is only interested in those characteristics that makes people subordinate. Examples of such characteristics include different skin color, a language foreign to the dominant population, and distinctive dress.

- -

Teacher's Comment:
I'm not sure that ignorance is quite the word you want to use in this paragraph. When I think of ignorance, I think of being unaware of something such as the different traits you are talking about. Later in the paragraph you say that "this group is only interested in those characteristics that makes people subordinate." This sentence makes me think that the dominant group is aware of the differences and chooses to discriminate based on

these differences rather than because they are ignorant of them. Please rethink this paragraph and decide whether you want to talk about ignorance or about choosing to discriminate.

We can contrast the previous example with this one, which is not text-specific.

Student's Text:

I like computers because they can help us a lot with our duties, and because they can give us some entertainment like the internet, where we can browse and check some websites, get interesting topics, check our emails, play games, and simply chat with our best friends who are in another country without spending so much money.

- -

Teacher's Comment (written right below the student's text):
Good, but could be better developed.

This teacher's comment could be written on any text, as it mentions nothing specific about this particular text. Additionally, and most important, the student cannot know from reading this comment what parts are good, what makes them good, what needs to be better developed, and what is meant by *better developed*. There is no direction for revision, nor is there anything from which the student can learn for this and future papers.

In fact, we can use text-specific comments as an opportunity for teaching. The following example is text-specific, but it doesn't give any "direction" for revision or do any teaching.

Student's Text:

Education is another strong influence. Traditionally boys are encouraged to learn mechanic, electronics and girls learn cooking, sewing. In an "active Device

Circuitry" classroom at Foothill college, Los Altos, male students are 98%. In the

meantime, 97% of female students are taking sewing class in the next classroom

- -

Teacher's Comment:
How does this tradition of what students are encouraged to
learn relate to current gender discrimination?

There are several concerns about this comment. First, the
question is an implied request for revision, asking the student
to explain the relationship between these details and gender
discrimination, and may not be interpreted as asking for revision (see Hyland & Hyland, 2001, for a further discussion of
implied requests). Second, the comment, while text-specific,
does not give any directions for revision or explain why what
the student has written does not achieve the purpose of this
paragraph. The comment could be rewritten as:

- -

Since you are trying to demonstrate that this educational tradition results in gender discrimination, you need to explain to
us <u>how</u> this tradition in education of separating boys and girls
into different classes results in gender discrimination. When you
claim that one thing causes or influences another, your reader is
going to want to know how that happens In addition, your discussion about what boys and girls are traditionally encouraged
to learn needs to show that there is a pattern, that is, that in
many educational situations boys are encouraged to learn what
are considered "masculine" subjects such as mechanics and girls
are encouraged to learn "feminine" subjects such as cooking and
sewing. If you don't show that this happens in many situations,
your reader will think that your example about Foothill is a
unique situation, that this doesn't happen in other places, and
thus gender discrimination is unique to Foothill. When you want
to show that something happens generally in a number of situations, you will need to show a pattern to do so.

In addition to text specificity, we can also consider the
syntactic shape of comments. On the whole, the research does

not suggest that the syntactic shape of a comment (whether or not the comment is phrased as a question, statement, or imperative) is directly related to whether or not students can understand the intent of a comment or how to revise in response to a comment. While Ferris (1997, 2001) did find that her subjects revised more successfully in response to information questions and imperatives and less successfully in response to comments that asked students to reconsider their thinking or arguments, she did not find that any one type of comment form unequivocally correlated with degree of revision success or whether or not a revision was attempted. Conrad and Goldstein (1999) found that neither the syntactic shape (whether the comments were questions, declaratives, or imperatives) nor their pragmatic shape (whether they were suggestions or directives) played a role in how effectively the subjects revised or whether or not they attempted revisions. In contrast, as in Ferris's studies, Conrad and Goldstein (1999) found that students had difficulty with comments that asked them to provide more of an explanation or a more effective explanation. Conrad and Goldstein (1999) suggest that this type of revision was less successful not because of the shape of the teacher's comments but because the students were developing their abilities to create and support arguments and needed further classroom instruction in doing so.

Since at this time there is no research to support the choice of one form of comment over another, teachers would be best served to see how their students work with the comments they actually use. For example, teachers might look to see if any patterns emerge that suggest that a particular type of comment does or does not cause confusion when they read their students' annotations about what they do and do not understand of the teacher's commentary. In doing this with my own students, I have noticed that certain questions and comments that I had hoped would get students to think more carefully about an argument or claim resulted instead in revisions where the students just added more details.

For example, in working with my student Tranh (see Conrad & Goldstein, 1999), I wrote comments that I intended to get him to think more carefully about his claims in hopes that he would either see that he could not support some of his claims or that he would explain or support his claims. I commented on one of his papers that *on page 2, paragraph 2, you say that having children affects a woman's job performance and career. You never explain how/why.* He revised by adding details about how pregnancy slows a woman's movements and causes anxiety and about women having to work long hours, rather than revising with explanation and argumentation. Tranh often interpreted questions and comments about how and why to mean "supply more information" rather than as a request to supply explanations. In retrospect, I could have written the previous comment as follows:

- -

> On page 2, paragraph 2, you say that having children affects a woman's job performance and career. In order to convince your reader that this happens, you need to describe how having children affects women and you need to explain how what happens to women when they have children negatively affects a woman's job performance and her career.

What I have done in the revised comment is avoid making a statement that only indirectly indicates a need for revision *(You never explain how/why)* while I have explained directly what Tranh needs to do to make his argument *(In order to convince your reader that this happens, you need to describe how having children affects women and you need to explain how what happens to women when they have children negatively affects a woman's job performance and her career).*

There is some evidence that in addition to indirectness, mitigation may, at least in some instances, also make it difficult for students to understand the intent of a teacher's comment (Conrad & Goldstein, 1999; Ferris, 1998; Hyland & Hyland, 2001). For example, in the comment *You might think about adding some details that show how the food appeared and tasted to whet your readers appetite,* a student could construe *might think about* to be signaling that this is something to consider but not all together necessary. In contrast, commenting *I understand that you would like your reader to want to try the foods you describe but without knowing exactly how they appeared and tasted, I didn't feel any strong desire to try these foods. Giving details of how the foods appear and taste would make me want to try them. Adding these details will help you achieve what you are trying to do in this section of your paper more directly shows the need for revision.*

Ferris (1999) also suggests that students can perceive a teacher's indirectness in his/her comments as a lack of confidence or competence. In addition, I have also worked with students who have "exploited" indirectness as a means to avoid making revisions. Some students have conveyed that if I write *might* or *could*, they decide that they do not "have to" make the revisions, and so they don't. Given all of these concerns, teachers should be very careful about how and when they mitigate their comments, or they should at the very least explain that mitigation is a politeness strategy that "softens" directives and does not imply an uncertainty about whether or not the teacher perceives a revision as a needed one.

Even if comment shape may not directly relate to revision success, certainly we have all experienced and have probably given commentary that is unclear. In the following example, too much is packed into a comment:

- -

Does Grimwade discuss these three groups? Why are you includ-ing this information here? How does his study relate to your own study? Does he ask similar questions that you ask? Does he begin research that you wish to build upon? Remember, in the literature review, you want to present information for your reader that is related to your topic in some way. Why are you including this particular study and all of the others here? Tell your reader.

In an interview with me, the student who received this comment told me that she understood the meaning of each individual sentence, but she didn't understand the comment as whole and what to do in response to it. In other instances, the language may be too technical, such as when a teacher uses technical words ("your paper lacks *cohesion* and *coherence*"), or the wording may be vague ("this paragraph is *awkwardly organized*"), or the comment may be written in language above the student's proficiency level. Thus, we need to plan our comments carefully and reread them, critically assessing their clarity.

Finally, we need to consider the tone of our comments. I remember years ago working with a teacher who was puzzled by her students' negative reaction to her. She asked me to sit in her classes and take a look at the feedback she was giving to her students. I noticed immediately that the tone of her feedback was derogatory. In one example, she wrote to a student, *Andrei, Andrei, how many times do I have to tell you....* If we consider the other examples in this chapter, we notice that those comments that point out what could make the text more effective are "neutral," and neither praise nor criticize. When we look at these neutral comments, we see that some point out to the writer where in the text there is a problem, some explain what the problem is, some give suggestions for how to revise, but none attack, belittle, or demean the writer or the writer's text.

Addressing What Students Need to Learn about Writing and about Texts

Some research has suggested that when students have difficulty revising, it is because of the type of problem needing revision and not because of the syntactic or pragmatic shape of the comment (Conrad & Goldstein, 1999; Ferris, 2001). The students in Conrad and Goldstein were able to successfully revise 90 percent of the problem areas other than development but successfully revised only 10 percent of the time for problems with argumentation, explanation, or analysis. Ferris (2001) also found that students were less successful revising problems with logic or argumentation. These studies suggest that students at the same level of writing proficiency in a class together may experience similar difficulties when composing.

Teachers, therefore, should look for patterns across students that they can address within the class for the group as whole. These lessons can address

- what the students may need to learn about some aspect of rhetoric
- how to read their writing critically to see if they are being rhetorically effective in respect to what is being learned
- appropriate revision strategies that can solve problems in the area under discussion.

Additionally, teachers should look for a student's patterns across papers for particular problem areas that can be addressed individually and monitored for progress.

While students need to learn revision strategies that can be used for particular types of problems, there is compelling evidence that commentary that provides strategies for revision may be particularly helpful to students (Conrad & Goldstein, 1999; Ferris, 1998; Goldstein & Kohls, 2002). Conrad and Goldstein suggest, for example, that the difficulties the students had with comments that focused on development might have been lessened if, along with comments they received that pointed out the problems in their texts, the students had been given strategies for revision. The following example from Ferris (2001) illustrates the difference between commentary with and without strategies:

> In one example, the teacher wrote the following comment: "you might consider what some psychologists have said about the impact of the situation on Jessica." To make this suggestion more concrete, the teacher perhaps could have said this instead: "In our readings, there were several statements from psychologists about what the effect on Jessica might be if she were returned to her birth parents. You might add a paragraph here which summarizes this information and discusses whether or not these expert opinions support your argument" (p. 313).

The teacher's actual comment gives no direction to the student about how to make the revision, and the student may wonder what it means to *consider* and then what to do after *considering*. In contrast, Ferris suggested rewording of the teacher's comment gives the student a clear strategy, sending the student back into the reading to review and summarize the psychologists' views and then back into the writing, showing the student how to use these views in the writing.

Putting It All Together: Planning for Response

The intent of this chapter has been to demonstrate that response is something that needs to be carefully planned and considered. Response is not grading or evaluating; it is a process of carefully reading what a student has written within the rhetorical context the student has created and communicated. Response needs to consider where the student is with the text, where the student needs to go, and where the student has been. It needs to be text-specific, understandable, and clear in its intent, and it needs to provide strategies for revision where appropriate. It needs to consider both what the student has communicated he or she needs help with and with what the teacher sees the student needing help; it needs to set priorities, avoiding overwhelming a student with too much feedback while targeting what would best help the student at that time given the needs of the student and the needs of the text. Response at its best guides a student to accomplish goals, praises the writer for what is effective, instructs for the current paper and future writing, and most important, shows the student that the teacher is actively and thoughtfully engaging in the reading of the student's paper. This chart summarizes the steps in written commentary.

WHAT TO RESPOND TO	*WHY*
➤ **TEXT**	
Student's questions and concerns as expressed on cover sheet/in annotations	Encourages student to read his/her work critically; provides help with what student feels he/she needs help.
Reader's difficulty understanding meaning at the sentence or text level	We write to convey meaning; it isn't possible to comment on what we do not understand.
Mismatch between purpose as stated in the student's cover note and how conveyed in the text	Allows the student to see how the text is being perceived and to make the decision about which accurately reflects the writer's purposes; avoids appropriating the student's text.
Aspect(s) of the text most in need of revision in order for the writer to fulfill purpose, meet audience needs, and/or genre needs	Treats every writer's text as a unique text in progress rather than as a final draft over which we have placed a template of what the text should look like.
Content	Writers write to convey meaning, and readers read to get this meaning from the text.
Emotions	Writers benefit from knowing that readers are relating to what they have written and what they have experienced.
What the writer is doing effectively	Plays a positive affective role and also teaches the student what is effective.
➤ **PROCESS**	
Student's processes for planning, generating text, evaluating text, revising, and finding content	The reasons behind problems in a text are not always evident from the text and may result from the processes a student uses.
➤ **REVISIONS**	
What students have revised successfully and less successfully using commentary and on their own	Allows students to learn from their revisions.

RESPONSE SHAPE	*WHY*
Either initial, within text, or terminal	No research suggests one more effective than the others; determine on a case-by-case basis, considering student preferences, nature of the text, and what needs to be revised.
Text-specific	Allows students to see exactly what needs revision or what is working well and why.
Direct (not mitigated)	Research suggests that students may not understand that mitigated comments are requests for revisions.
Include revision strategies	Research suggests that including revision strategies helps students understand how to revise and why; students can apply such strategies to future texts.
Respect student preferences	Students have preferences for what types of comments they work well with.
Avoid comment types students find confusing	Comments that are not text-specific, are overly complex, vaguely worded, and/or too technical can be difficult to understand and use productively.
Use neutral tone for aspects of the text needing revision	Comments worded with a negative tone are demeaning and nonproductive.
Teach through commentary	Providing instruction through commentary allows teachers to individualize instruction; it also allows students to see how advice and strategies can be applied to similar issues in future texts.

Chapter 4

Reflective Teaching and Teacher Research

Years ago, while I was pursuing my doctorate, one of my professors made a statement about teaching experience that has remained with me: A teacher who has been teaching for ten years might have ten years of experience or might only have one year, repeated ten times. Certainly, we all strive to grow through experience, to have that ten years of experience rather than the same one year repeated over and over. It is my intent in this chapter to share ways that teachers can reflect on and use their experiences giving feedback and helping students revise and write more effectively so that these experiences are meaningful and accumulative and teacher practices are modified when modification is needed. In addition, this chapter encourages teachers to carry out close examinations of their practices and to share these examinations with others, so that we can build a more complete picture of teacher commentary and student revision than what currently exists.

Reflective Teaching

The movement within the L2 teaching field toward reflective teaching, informed practice, and teacher research informs my views. Richards and Lockhart (1994) and Bailey (1997) caution against a reliance on experience to foster teacher growth; Bailey et al. (1996) further caution that often "we teach as we have been taught" (p.11). Instead of a sole reliance on experience to inform our practices, Richards and Lockhart advocate a process of reflection: "In asking and answering questions...teachers are in a position to evaluate their teaching, to decide if aspects of their own teaching could be changed, to develop strategies for change, and to monitor the effects of completing these strategies" (p. 2). In looking at the assumptions underlying teacher reflection, Richards and Lockhart also discuss how teachers are often not aware of exactly what they are doing. Reflection allows us to become aware. As Bailey (1997) points out in her discussion of reflective teaching, "the process of reflecting on the data...can enable us to uncover what is not intuitively obvious. The data can nudge us out of our comfortable impressions of our own teaching by making us look with fresh eyes at the record of events that occur in our classrooms" (p. 11). We can see that what is crucial to reflection is the "critical" analyses of our practices, analyses that allow us to understand what underlies our practices, how effective our practices are, and what our students' reactions to our practices are. These analyses also allow us to envision ways of altering our practices to make them more effective.

I have learned important lessons from reflective teaching and from my research on my own teaching (for published accounts, see Goldstein & Conrad, 1990, and Conrad & Goldstein, 1999). One lesson came from Bingo, the student I wrote about in Chapter 3, who had annotated his writing. His annotations made me realize that I had been missing an important part of the process of teacher commentary and student revision—that is, knowing what the writer thought about his/her paper and where the writer felt help/feedback was needed. I realized that I had, in essence, been commenting in a vacuum. Thus I began to explore whether or not knowing what the writer thought about his/her paper and what the writer felt was needed from me led me to provide more effective feedback and led to better revisions by my students. As a result, I began to ask my students to annotate their texts, and I used these annotations while reading and responding to their texts. I discovered that the students' annotations helped me avoid appropriating their texts and helped me respond more effectively. I discovered that students directly benefited from the process of annotation because this process encouraged them to be critical readers of their own writing and asked them to take more responsibility for their writing because they had to think carefully about where revision or help was needed.

My research on teacher feedback grew directly out of my concern for understanding what my students actually did with my feedback and whether or not I needed to change my practices. Some of the advice I share in this book is a result of this research. One very important lesson for me was the discovery of how complex the feedback process is and how many factors outside the teacher's commentary play a role in how students use feedback. I now understand how much the factors that students bring to the processes of writing and revising affect how they use teacher commentary and how they revise.

For example, Marigrace waited for my feedback and followed it diligently, even when she really didn't understand it or agree with it. Never did she revise on her own or question any of my comments, for she believed that her role was to do what I told her and my role was to tell her what to do. Tranh had strong beliefs he wanted to convey even in the face of contradictory evidence, and he lacked the strategies for finding appropriate evidence to bolster his points of views. Zohre was overwhelmed by all that she had to accomplish outside our class, which affected the quantity and degree of complexity of her revisions. Now I always consider the individual and look for the factors that might play a role in each of my student's writing and revisions. I also learned that, for these three students, what I commented on played a significant role in how well they revised. Since they were still struggling with how to develop arguments, my comments on their arguments were either not used or, when used, the resulting revisions not successful. Thus, I could see that I needed to work in class with these students on argumentation. From this, I have learned to look for and build a connection between classroom instruction, my feedback, and my students' revisions. In addition, by examining how Marigrace, Tranh, and Zohre used my feedback, I learned to avoid *how* and *why* questions since they were often misinterpreted just as being "food for thought" rather than requests for revision. Instead, I now explain why I am asking these questions and how answering them can strengthen the student's text. Based on conversations with Tranh and with

Hoshiko, I learned never to assume I know why a student did not revise or had difficulty revising but to ask why the student was having difficulty. Talking with Tranh, I learned what strategies he used to generate support and how these strategies interfered with his finding effective support. Talking with Hoshiko, I learned that she did not know how to do a certain type of citation and therefore needed to learn how to do so before she could effectively use her teacher's feedback.

Possibilities for Reflection

There are many questions a teacher might ask about the process within which teachers provide written commentary to students about their writing and within which students use this commentary in their revisions. We can examine the context, the teacher, the student(s), the comments, the types of areas commented on, and the revisions, and we can examine a range of interactions among these variables. In the following section, I will address a few of the possible questions to illustrate the processes that teachers can undertake in examining teacher commentary and student revision. These processes allow for reflection on what works, how to make changes where needed, and how to examine the degree to which the changes have improved on practice. The questions, while by no means exhaustive, grow out of my experiences as a teacher, teacher educator, and researcher. They are a starting point, rather than an ending point. While they may be consistent with things you have also noticed or wondered about, or to which you have sought answers, you may have other questions to add.

The Nature of What Is and Is Not Commented On

What do I comment on?
What do I not comment on?

Teachers can begin by asking themselves what beliefs shape what they choose to comment on and what they choose not to comment on. In doing so, teachers can also ask what factors, if any, they believe play a role in their choices. Some factors that might affect what teachers choose to comment on are *genre, content of the writing, time in the semester, previous issues in students' papers, type/level of student, programmatic expectations or requirements, individual student characteristics, attitudes toward different students, which draft the teacher is commenting on, what students have written in annotations to their texts, and particular types of rhetorical issues/problems.*

Teachers can first take a set of student papers and notice exactly what they comment on, and they can then organize their comments into categories to identify patterns. Possible ways to categorize to what teachers respond include *the type of rhetorical problem, issues being discussed in class, previous difficulties a student has evidenced in previous papers, rhetorical aspects that the next course in the program expects students to have mastered, and/or problems identified by students for which they have requested feedback.*

Next, teachers can create coding charts for themselves to help them code comments for each student:

A. What I Commented On

Student "X"	Comment 1	Comment 2	Comment 3	Comment 4	Comment 5	Comment 6	Comment 7	Comment 8
Rhetorical Features:								
Organization								
Development								
Genre requirements								
Audience								
Purpose								
Cohesion								
Coherence								
Aspect discussed in class								
Program expects "control" of this aspect								
Student request								
Previous difficulty with this aspect								
Problem with content								

This page is reproducible.

Teachers can also chart the parts of the student's text on which they did not comment:

B. What I Did Not Comment On:								
Student "X"	Text Portion A	Text Portion B	Text Portion C	Text Portion D	Text Portion E	Text Portion F	Text Portion G	Text Portion H
Rhetorical Features:								
Organization								
Development								
Genre requirements								
Audience								
Purpose								
Cohesion								
Coherence								
Aspect discussed in class								
Program expects "control" of this aspect								
Student request								
Previous difficulty with this aspect								
Problem with content								

The next step depends on what question(s) a teacher is trying to answer. For example, if teachers want to know to what extent they are commenting on a particular rhetorical area in students' papers, they would concentrate their analyses by looking at the columns that focus on that rhetorical feature. Thus, a teacher might want to compare how often he/she responds to issues of purpose and audience. Here the teacher can count how often he/she responded to each of these rhetorical features for each student and in total for all students. Such quantification will also help teachers to see patterns in terms of whether particular features are commented on more frequently than others across the group as a whole, as well as for each student.

However, quantification should not be the end of the process. Teachers next need to reflect on what they have found, asking themselves the following questions by looking at the patterns they uncover as well as their comments and the students' texts:

1. What patterns do I see in what I comment on?
2. What do the patterns I uncover indicate to me about what I focus on when I comment?
3. Why do I think I comment in the way I do as indicated by my analyses?
4. Do the patterns indicate a systematic approach to what I comment on or an unsystematic approach?
5. If they indicate a systematic approach, what is this approach, and does it make pedagogical sense to me?
6. What patterns do I see in what I do not comment on?
7. What reasons account for what I have not commented on?
8. Do I feel these are sound reasons?
9. Did I treat students differently? If so, what accounts for having done so? Are there sound reasons for having done so?

The process does not stop here. Depending on what teachers have seen in their analyses of comments, they may decide that certain aspects are not as they would like them to be. This calls for planning an action to change whatever it is that they feel is not as effective or sound as it should be. In one instance, a teacher may notice that the comments only focus on aspects of students' texts that are easy to revise such as adding details. In thinking about why, this teacher may realize that he/she felt afraid that the students might have difficulty with more challenging revisions such as providing explanations. Thus, in the next round of commenting, the teacher could choose to comment on a particular problem area with which many students are having difficulty and to which the teacher has not commented on previously because of concerns for how well the students could use the comments. This, of course, would lead to another round of examination focusing on how well students were able to revise using these comments. On one hand, the teacher might find that, contrary to previous concerns, students were able to use these comments to revise successfully. On the other hand, the teacher might find the students were not able to revise successfully, and, in response, design class sessions to address these rhetorical issues and revisions of such problems. (See pages 114–116 for discussion on how to analyze revision success.)

Teachers can also look at what they have not commented on. For example, a teacher may find that the comments do not address those elements the students have indicated they would like help with. In the next round of commentary, the teacher can provide such comments, and then, in the next round of coding, examine the degree to which he/she has done so. Finally, the teacher can see how successfully the students have used commentary on areas the students have self-selected and, if they find students are having difficulty doing so, lead a class discussion about the reasons why.

The Nature of Comments: What Shape Do My Comments Take?

The research on teacher commentary has looked at what forms teacher's comments take and, in particular, the syntactic shape, pragmatic intent, text specificity, directness, tone, and suggestions for revision (see Chapter 3 for a discussion of this research). Teachers can examine the shape of their commentary, looking at one or more of these categories to see what forms their commentary take. The following recommendations[1] allow teachers to categorize their comments in terms of not only what they have focused on but also the tone of the comments, the directness of the comments, the linguistic form of the comments, the function of the comments, and the text specificity of the comments.

Analyzing Feedback

Analyze your comments in terms of **WHAT YOU FOCUS ON, TONE** (praise, criticism, neutral tone), **DIRECTNESS** (direct, hedged), **FUNCTION** (ask for information, provide information, provide instruction, ask for revision, give instruction for revision, teacher correct or rewrite directly, direct student to do something other than revision [for example, read something], offer praise, offer criticism), **LINGUISTIC FORM** (question, statement, imperative, exclamation), and **TEXT SPECIFICITY** (text-specific, non–text specific). Keep in mind that some comments might be coded for more than one characteristic within one category.

Comment #	What You Focus On	Tone	Directness	Function	Linguistic Form	Text Specificity
1						
2						
3						
4						
5						
6						
7						
8						

While this chart allows teachers to categorize all of their comments across all of these categories, teachers can create their own charts in which they use only one or a few of these

---

[1]This chart is adapted from my colleague John Hedgcock.

categories depending on what each teacher would like to know at any one point in time. For example, a teacher may be interested in knowing whether or not comments are text specific and thus may go through student papers and categorize comments in terms of text specificity. In this particular example, once the categorization is completed, a teacher can analyze a number of different aspects concerning text specificity. The first pass-through may only look at the degree to which comments are text specific. Once a teacher has completed these numerical analyses, the next step is to ask what any differences mean. Let's imagine, for example, that a teacher finds that she/he provides text-specific comments in about half of the comments. This teacher can then ask whether or not the differences are warranted and whether or not they make pedagogical sense. In order to answer this question, the teacher needs to look at the instances where the comments are text specific and where they are not and see if any patterns emerge. Perhaps places where comments are not text specific address text issues that the teacher and student have discussed in conference and there is shared knowledge that obviates the need for text specificity. Or, in contrast, perhaps the teacher uncovers that the lack of text specificity in some places seems not to be patterned or patterned in a way that doesn't make pedagogical sense. Here, from going through this process, the teacher can now formulate a plan for how to use text specificity in his/her next round of commentary and then undertake a new round of analyses.

Teachers can also consider what exactly they would like to know about their use of text specificity. For example, a teacher might decide to look at whether different students receive different amounts of text-specific comments, or whether different types of problems are treated differently in terms of how often they receive text-specific comments, or whether different drafts of a paper receive different amounts of text-specific comments. Teachers would again categorize their comments in terms of text specificity; then compare students, problems, or drafts in terms of the quantity of text-specific comments and finally ask what any similarities or differences mean in these comparisons and whether such differences are warranted. If a teacher feels such differences are not warranted, the teacher can make changes and begin the process of inquiry again to examine what happens after these changes.

The Interaction between Commentary and Revision

A crucial question teachers have is whether or not their commentary helps students to revise their work and make their papers stronger. The process for examining this entails looking at the relationship between commentary and revision. There is very little published research that looks at this (see, for example, Conrad & Goldstein, 1999). Such research tends to look at the whole picture; it categorizes all of the commentary across a wide range of categories, and it looks at all of the revisions across several papers and across multiple drafts of each paper. It then codes these revisions as successful or not, as well as coding places where commentary was given but revision not undertaken. It finally looks for relationships among the different comment categories and whether revision is successful, unsuccessful, or not attempted. I know from personal experience that such research is extremely time consuming and may not be feasible within the time constraints of the typical workday of an L2 writing teacher. There are, however, many questions that can be answered by looking at parts of the picture and that are more feasible for teachers to address. Teachers may want to know whether or not text specificity helps students revise, whether or not providing specific revision strategies is helpful, or whether phrasing comments as questions or statements makes a difference in the success of students' revisions. Some teachers may want to know what attitudes and expectations their students have to particular types of comments, and in turn whether such reactions and attitudes mediate the students' use of such comments.

Once teachers have decided what aspect of their commentary they are interested in analyzing in relation to student revision, they need to look at their comments and categorize them for that aspect. The chart and process discussed previously (pp. 111–114) will help teachers to do this first part. The next step entails categorizing revisions as successful, not successful, or not attempted. *Not attempted* is straightforward—the student has not revised the text where the teacher has provided commentary. In contrast, the successful and unsuccessful labels are more subjective. In my own work, I have defined *success* as a revision that, in response to the commentary, improves on the student's text given the student's purpose and audience. I believe it is crucial to contextualize the notion of success so that it takes into account what the writer is trying to do, for what purpose, and for whom. We neither write in a rhetorical vacuum nor revise in a rhetorical vacuum, and each writer's rhetorical context will be different from every other writer's. Thus, commentary needs to be provided within the writer's context, a context that the writer has made known to the teacher through cover notes or text annotations (see Chapter 3 for a discussion of cover notes and text annotations), and revision needs to take place within this context as well. If we use this notion of success, we can also see that revisions can be more or less successful. That is, some revisions may completely solve the rhetorical problem, but others, while improving the text, may not completely solve the problem. For this reason, some may want to code student revisions as unsuccessful, partially successful, and completely successful.

After both types of coding are completed—the categorization of comments and the coding of success of revisions—teachers are now ready to look for the relationships between comment characteristic(s) and revision success. Now teachers can consider whether students revise more or less successfully in response to comments that have whatever characteristic they have chosen to analyze, such as text specificity or the provision of revision strategies or directness, for example.

Whatever patterns exist need to also be understood in light of what students tell us they have done with our commentary. In Chapter 2 we discussed having students keep revision journals in which they detail what revisions they made and why, which they did not make and why, and what difficulties they encountered using our comments and why. These journals are fertile ground for understanding what students do when they use our comments to revise. Teachers can look through these journals to see whether or not students have commented on what has made comments easy or difficult to use and see what light such entries shed on the patterns they are finding between commentary characteristics and revision success. In my research I have also interviewed students, asking them to describe how they have used their teacher's comments and the concerns and difficulties they have had and why. Teachers can also do this as a means of understanding what in their commentary students find helpful or not helpful. Another alternative is to show students the patterns of relationship the teacher has found between a particular comment characteristic and degree of revision success and ask the students what they think explains this relationship.

Thus, what teachers will have are many types of data with which to work—their students' cover notes or text annotations, their coding of comments for particular characteristics, their coding of students' revisions in terms of how successfully the revisions improve the students' texts, and their students' insights about what works and does not work for them when using their teachers' comments for revision. Examining these sources of data together will allow teachers to deepen their understanding of the crucial relationship between commentary and revision. In turn, this type of reflection will enable teachers to ask new questions about the relationship between other comment characteristics and revision and to make changes in their practice to bring about more effective revision.

Other Areas for Research

The previous discussions have focused on three crucial areas for reflective teaching: *what is commented on, what shape the comments take, and the relationships between what is commented and revision success or what shape comments take and revision success.*

While these questions grow out of my experiences as a teacher, teacher educator, and researcher, they are, however, not exhaustive. Reflective teaching means thinking deeply about one's own context and posing the questions that need to be asked within that context. My intention in the previous section was to detail some of the questions that can be asked and how for some we might go about answering them. In a more general sense, we can follow the list of questions that Patterson and Shannon (1993, cited in Arias, 1995) offer to aid teachers in carrying out their reflections:

- What specifically am I doing in my classroom?
- What does it mean that I choose to do it this way?
- How are the students responding?
- What does it mean that they respond this way?
- How did I come to do and see things this way?
- What do I intend to change and how? (p. 65)

While the suggestions I offer for teacher reflection and research encompass some of the central concerns, teachers and researchers can ask other questions as well. In my paper on the state of research about teacher commentary (Goldstein, 2001), I reviewed the studies about written response to L2 writers that had been published as of 1999 (the reviews encompassed 15 studies published between 1985 and 1999). My review noted that much of the research reported was largely noncontextual and that it had not taken into account social factors; had focused largely on texts; and had not looked closely at the many factors that can interact as students write, teachers comment, and students revise using these comments. Chapter 1 of this book discusses many of these factors and the need to look at the process of composing, commentary, and revision contextually. These concerns lead to a number of questions that research can address:

- What is the relationship between classroom instruction and what teachers comment on?
- What is the relationship between classroom instruction and what students revise and how well students revise?

- What is the relationship between students' attitudes toward types of commentary and revision success?
- What are students able to revise on their own without teacher commentary?
- Does type of genre, topic, point in the semester, or draft play a role in what students revise and how well they revise using teacher commentary?
- What effect does context have on commentary? That is, do instructional and/or programmatic attitudes or requirements affect what teachers respond to or how they respond?
- What effect does context have on students' revisions? That is, do instructional and/or programmatic attitudes or requirements affect what they revise or how well they revise using commentary?
- Are there individual student factors (e.g., time constraints; investment in the course or the topic or writing; prior good or negative experiences with writing; beliefs about what makes writing effective; beliefs about who is responsible, teacher or student, for revision) that affect how well students revise using commentary?
- What are the longitudinal effects of teacher commentary and students' revision on student writing and student-motivated revision?
- How do the roles that teachers play as readers (e.g., editor, expert, peer, audience, gatekeeper) influence how they comment, how students perceive their commentary, and how students use their commentary? (See Sperling, 1994, for research in L1 composition on teacher roles and teacher commentary.)
- In what ways do the following influence the roles that teachers adopt as readers: student characteristics, attitudes toward different students, the content of what students write about, text features, institutional or programmatic demands?
- What do teachers not comment on in comparison to what teachers do comment on, and what are the underlying motivations of these choices?

- How is teacher commentary used within the whole process of revision—that is, what do students revise on their own, what do they use teacher's commentary for when revising, and how successful are they in each of these types of revision?

Sharing Research

I have mentioned throughout this book the dearth of research on teacher commentary and student revision. Certainly this is due, at least in part, to the time it takes to do such research. Nonetheless, this research is crucial to our understanding of the process of teacher commentary and student revision. For this reason, I would like to encourage teachers to not only undertake reflective teaching but to also disseminate their findings from these small-scale investigations. There are many avenues for dissemination—conversations among teachers; teacher meetings on campus; local conferences; and larger conferences such as TESOL, AAAL, or CCCC; as well as in electronic or print publications. I would also like to encourage teachers and researchers to explore the additional questions that I have posed in the previous section.

Some may argue or be afraid that such small-scale studies are not useful because they are not generalizable. However, no study, quantitative or qualitative, small or large, case study or experimental, is really generalizable. Every time we study something, we need to do so within its unique context, and since no two contexts are identical, no study can ever be completely generalizable to any other context. Instead, generalizabilty, or in a sense an understanding of the whole picture, can only be built by amassing many sound small studies that look at the broad range of questions about teacher commentary and revision and do so across a wide range of contexts. We can develop the whole picture if we can read, compare, and discuss a multitude of studies.

Conducting Sound Research

In Goldstein (2001), I critique the published studies on teacher commentary and student revision. In particular, I note problems with methodology and problems with sufficiently detailed reporting. My intent here is to share these findings so that those who carry out research will do so in a sound manner and report research in a comprehensive manner.

First, in doing research we need to avoid confounding variables. Some previous research has grouped together students working under different conditions without considering the effect of these differing situations. We need to avoid, for example, treating as the same students who wrote about different topics, who revised in class versus outside of class, who were writing and revising in different pedagogical contexts, or who were writing within different genres. Since we can assume that any of these factors may affect how teachers comment and how students revise with this commentary, it is very important that researchers use appropriate research controls.

We need to use appropriate research methodologies. I list here some of the methodological problems I have seen in research so that researchers can avoid these problems:

- What students say they do with commentary is not the same as what they actually do with commentary. If researchers would like to know what students actually do with commentary, they need to examine actual student texts and not just rely on student self-reports.
- When we code teacher comments, we need to be careful not to assume we know the teachers' motivations for the shape or content of comments. If we want to know the intention, we need to ask. In the same vein, when students revise using teacher commentary, if we want to know the reasons for how they used the comments, we have to use methodologies that allow students to tell us why they did what they did.

- In order to understand how individual student character-istics affect how students use teacher commentary while revising, we need to do case studies instead of studies with large numbers of subjects so that we can see the richness of each student's experience.
- If we want to know something about the role of comment shape, we need to use the appropriate coding methodolo-gies. Thus, if we want to know what happens when stu-dents revise using comments phrased as questions, then we need to code for this.
- If we want to know how teacher commentary helps stu-dents to improve their drafts and writing, we need to de-velop sound definitions of improvement and then examine students' texts using these definitions.
- In contrast, we need to avoid assigning scores to drafts written before and after commentary as our sole measure of improvement since scores can only tell us that a text is better or not but not how or why. In addition, changes in scores may reflect myriad influences including, but not limited to, teacher commentary.
- If we want to discover if a teacher is treating students fairly with his/her commentary, we need to move beyond just looking at what the teacher commented on and how. We need to also look at what the teacher could have com-mented on but didn't, the nature of the student's text and the issues within it, and the nature of past texts and text issues for each student. What may appear to be biased or unsystematic commentary may turn out to be appropriate and systematic when we see the full picture. For example, if we see that a teacher only responded to sentence-level errors in one student's paper, but responded to rhetorical issues in another student's paper, we might conclude that the students were being treated in an unsystematic way. However, if we looked at each paper and saw that the one where the teacher responded only to sentence-level errors had no rhetorical problems while the other student's paper did, we would see that the responses were appropriate and systematic.

We also need to make sure we collect sufficient data to answer whatever our research question is. Many studies only examine one text, or one draft of a text, or only the texts that were written at the beginning of the semester. What data we need to collect and how much of course depends on the research question we are asking, but we do need to make sure the data is sufficient to answer this question. If we want to know how students work with teacher commentary over time, we will need to collect their texts over time; if we want to know the relationship between genre and what teachers comment on, we will need to look at a variety of genres. If we are interested in discovering how a student's individual characteristics affect how he/she uses teacher commentary, we will need to look at all of that student's work over a semester, as these characteristics may affect how the student uses commentary differently at different points in a semester, for different assignments, or different contents, in fact for many different variables.

Reporting Research

In reviewing published research on teacher commentary, I have also found that many studies are insufficiently detailed. This is problematic for a number of reasons.

- *Validity and reliability:* In order to feel confident of a study's findings, we need to feel confident that the researcher has used the appropriate subjects, has collected appropriate and sufficient data, and has employed the appropriate methods for collecting and analyzing the data. Thus, research reports need to provide a sufficiently detailed report of the subjects, the data, research methods, and methods of analyses.
- *Context:* In order to understand what the results of a study mean, we need to have a full understanding of the context within which the research was conducted. There is no such thing as a standard context, as the nexus of variables within a setting uniquely defines contexts: the

institution, the teacher, the student, the texts, the contents, the type of program, and the pedagogical approach. Researchers need to give full descriptions of context so that those who are reading their studies can truly understand what the findings mean. For example, a study may find that students prefer grammatical comments to rhetorical comments. The true meaning of this finding will only be revealed, however, if we know the context within which the students are working. If in this context the teacher stresses grammatical accuracy given his/her belief that this is what should be commented on first and foremost, we can see that the students may have taken on this value from how the teacher comments. But if the teacher is not at all concerned with grammatical accuracy and never comments on it, then we can see that the students have certain beliefs about and desires for types of commentary that may be separate from the teacher's pedagogical practices.

- *Comparability:* As mentioned earlier in this chapter, a deeper understanding of teacher commentary and student revision awaits the accumulation of many studies in many different contexts that allow us to see the interaction between and among all of the factors that can affect the processes of commenting and revising. Our ability to fully understand this can only come if we can compare across studies, and we can only compare across studies if they are fully detailed. For example, two studies may show that two different teachers comment in very different ways. On the face of it, we might surmise that these two teachers were behaving in very different ways related to personal idiosyncrasies. However, if we have enough detail to see that each teacher commented from the perspective of what he/she expected students to already know how to revise, then we can begin to see that in fact these two teachers were behaving in similar ways. Thus, in order for us to be able to compare across studies, researchers need to provide sufficient detail for readers about the context, the students, the teacher, the texts (including contents, genre, drafts, point in the semester), the commentary, the revisions, and the methodologies for data collection and data analysis.

Conclusion

My hope is that this chapter has empowered readers to critically reflect on their practices as they provide feedback to their students and to make whatever changes they feel would improve on their practices in helping students revise and become more effective writers. Beyond this, however, my hope is that teachers and researchers will begin to conduct studies that answer the many questions that remain largely unexamined about teacher commentary and student revision. It is essential that these studies be undertaken and that teachers and researchers disseminate what they learn so that we can develop a full picture across many contexts of the processes of commentary and revision.

Chapter 5

Educating Pre- and In-Service Second Language Composition Teachers

Helping teachers develop sound and effective methods for responding to their students' writing is one of the most challenging aspects of working with pre-service and in-service teachers of L2 composition. The students in the master's-level course I teach on teaching L2 writing have shared with me how difficult they find the process of giving feedback to be. The in-service teachers I have worked with over the years echo this difficulty. This chapter, therefore, addresses how teacher educators might work with teachers, pre- and in-service alike, to help them develop their abilities to give sound written responses to their writing students.

Preliminaries: Process, Product, and Genre

In Chapter 3, we looked at how teachers can respond not only to students' texts but also to the writer's composing processes and intervene where a student's processes are not effective. However, when students indicate these difficulties in their revision journals, in order for teachers to respond, they need to first understand what we mean by composing processes. Many pre- and in-service teachers I have worked with initially have the mistaken notion that composing processes are linear, that it means following the ordered steps of *write, reread, and edit.* I have found that teachers thus benefit from reading some of the published literature on cognitive and social approaches to writing processes[1] (see, for example, Cooper, 1986; Faigley, 1986; Flower, 1979; Harris, 1989; Krapels, 1990; Raimes, 1985; Rose, 1980; Zamel, 1983) and that they benefit from introspective analyses of their own writing processes as they compose. For example, in my course on the teaching of writing to second language students, I ask my students to keep a journal as they write a paper for any other course that they are taking that semester and write an account of the process of writing the paper. The assignment follows:

Description of Your Own Processes/Essay

Chose a writing assignment you have for **another class** this semester—in particular, one you can begin now or near this time. For our course, you will keep a journal and then write a report based on your journal notes that details the process you go through in writing this paper. Please use the questions that follow to guide your journal and your report. As part of this experience you will also conference with the professor of the teaching-of-writing course, and you will work throughout with a peer coach. This will entail doing the following:

A. Clear paper choice with the professor of the teaching-of-writing course

B. Write first draft*

C. Work on subsequent drafts*

D. Meet with peer coach for feedback (at whatever point you feel is most beneficial)

---

[1]Here I do not intend process to be equated to "expressionism," "a model of learning based on individual motivation, personal freedom, self-expression, and learner responsibility" (Hyland, 2003, p. 19.) By *process,* I mean a focus on the cognitive processes of composing, the plans, strategies, and heuristics writers utilize as they plan, compose, and revise, and social notions of process encompassing considerations such as the expectations of particular discourse communities and genres.

E. Schedule an appointment with and meet with the professor of the teaching- of-writing course for feedback (at whatever point you feel is most beneficial)

F. Repeat steps C–E as needed/desired

G. Finish paper

As you are writing (and incubating), you need to keep track of what you are doing, where, when, and why. Keep notes on the following:

1. What methods did you use to get started (ways in/heuristics)?

2. How did you write your first draft (where, when, how long; did you plan, reread, rewrite, or evaluate at any point; where and why)?

3. What concerns did you have as you began your first draft?

4. What concerns did you have as you wrote your second draft?

5. How did you write your second draft (see questions in #2)?

6. What changes resulted from your revisions of your first draft? Why did you make these changes? How did you feel about them?

7. If you wrote more drafts before your final draft, answer questions 4–6 about these drafts.

8. Answer questions 4, 5, & 6 for your final draft.

9. What role did peer responses play in your revision process?

10. What role did the conference with the teacher play in your revision process?

11. What role did your content teacher's comments play in the revision process?

12. What conclusions do you reach about your composing processes?

13. Has the process of doing this paper changed your attitudes toward writing or your writing processes? What has changed and why?

You will submit a paper incorporating your answers to the previous questions, as well as the paper through which you examined your processes.

* I use the term "draft" loosely; some will find themselves having discernible, separate drafts, while others will notice that as they work on their papers that it is difficult to "see" separate drafts. There is no need to change how you write: When you give your paper to a peer to read or to the teacher, just give us what you have at that particular time.

The readings and teachers' introspections about their own processes allow them to understand and discuss what is meant by process, what difficulties L2 writers might have with writing processes, and what possible helpful interventions and heuristics are available for solving these problems that might be suggested in teachers' feedback to their students. For example, we might talk about L2 writers who indicate in their process journals that they stop and read every sentence because of a premature concern for accuracy and therefore lose the sense of coherence in their text. We could then move on to talking about heuristics that we might suggest in our written feedback to help a student deal with this type of difficulty.

In addition, teachers need to understand *product*, that is, what "shapes" writing takes in particular discourse communities and why (Hyland, 2004), and what rhetorical strategies are available to writers to achieve their purposes within a discourse community for a particular audience, topic, and genre. Writing teachers cannot possibly identify what their students need help with or give them this help through written feedback without some understanding of what rhetoric and genre are and how audience, topic, and purposes interact within a discourse community to shape writing. To this end, teachers would benefit from reading about genre, audience and purpose, rhetoric, and discourse communities (see, e.g., Hyland, 2000; Johns, 2002; Ramanathan & Kaplan,

2000; Swales, 1990). Additionally, some time could be spent on doing analyses of selected texts. Here teachers would examine what discourse community the texts were written within, who the audience(s) is/are, what the topics are, what the purpose(s) is/are and how these influence text structure, the types of development, the types of organizational patterns (if relevant), the types of evidence, the nature of the lexicon and syntactic patterns, and so forth. For example, students might choose articles from different discourse communities and complete this assignment:

Discourse Analysis of Published Work in Your Discourse Community

You will write an analysis of and be prepared to discuss in class two representative published pieces in your discourse community. Your analysis should answer the following questions and give examples from the text to illustrate your answers. Make sure to bring the article as well as your answers to the questions.

1. Who is the intended audience? What assumptions does the author make about the intended audience in terms of new and old information? Beliefs/opinions? Goals for reading? Other?

2. What is (are) the purpose(s) of the piece?

3. What is the topic and thesis of the piece? How does audience and purpose influence topic and thesis?

4. What is the genre (literature review, research report, critique, etc.)? How does audience and purpose influence genre?

5. Describe the organizational framework.

6. How is the piece developed? What types of development are used?

7. What type of introduction and what type of conclusion is used?

8. How is third person "unknown" referred to?

9. What style does the author use for internal citations? References? Quotes? Footnotes?

10. Describe the nature of the vocabulary and syntax used (consider style, tone, register).

11. How does audience and purpose influence the text structure and form (types of organization and development, introduction and conclusion, lexical and grammatical choices)?

The purpose of doing this is not to exhaustively cover all possible discourse communities, which of course is not possible, but to model for teachers the process by which one analyzes and learns about texts within different discourse communities. In that way, as teachers work with different groups of L2 writers, they will have the tools to teach themselves about each rhetorical context and the nature of texts within these contexts.

Pre-Service Teachers: Learning about Response as a Whole Class

I have found that teachers feel insecure about their abilities to give effective written feedback and that they both welcome and benefit from spending time in class discussing principles that govern written feedback as well as working together to practice giving written feedback. One starting point is having teachers reflect about the types of feedback they have received, how they feel about these different types of feedback, and what their preferences are. For example, in my class, I ask my graduate students to respond to the following questions and to post their responses to our class e-mail folder:

Individual Feedback Attitudes: What are the different types of feedback you have received on your writing? What types of feedback do you like/prefer? Why? What types of feedback do you dislike? Why? What would be your "ideal" feedback? Answer these questions, post your responses to the e-mail folder, and be prepared to discuss in class.

These introspections remind my students and me every semester how much they already know about response and allow us as a class to bring our ideas together to create a list of good feedback practices. Thus, for example, one semester we learned from Donna that her ideal feedback would be "based more on content than on language. There would hopefully be equal amounts of positive feedback and helpful suggestions, and those helpful suggestions would ideally be positively worded (e.g., instead of saying, 'You have completely misunderstood Bachman's model of communicative competence,' my reviewer would find a kinder, gentler way to point out my lack of understanding)." Barbara added a concern for learning from feedback, that she wanted it "to teach. It's nice to feel like they're trying to help me learn through their feedback, instead of tell me what I didn't learn." Vincent brought in the concern for appropriation: "Although T written feedback is my preferred way, the one I dislike is when the feedback reflects the ideas, opinions or interpretations of the Ts themselves (or reader/corrector). I remember writing a paper once where all the feedback I received reflected the point of view of my instructor. She paid no attention to what I had to say, at my interpretations, and provided no quality feedback or guidance for my paper." Karen recognized the role and importance of audience: "I'd say this experience changed my perspectives on feedback forever. When we talk about the readers' interaction with text—I understand all too well. Nothing is more liberating (and eye-opening) than to hear others interpret your writing when you cannot explain what you meant...." Mary reminded us to be text-specific and to provide suggestions: "I prefer feedback that is specific rather than vague. I also appreciate legible and insightful feedback. When people give me specific, legible, and insightful feedback complemented by their suggestions, I am more willing to accept and comprehend the nature of the feedback. For example, if people are telling me to expand an idea, I would like to know the idea they are referring to, followed by specific suggestions (e.g., you can expand this ____ idea by using ____ researcher's idea such as ____). When feedback is vague, I become increasingly frustrated trying to interpret what the reader is trying to tell me. I also prefer direct (and constructive) rather than indirect feedback. Nothing makes me more agitated than a passive-aggressive reader." Finally, Jonathan reminded us to offer praise and to be critical but respectful by using comments that are constructive. To him this "includes positive 'back slapping' comments because they let the writer know what he or she is doing well and to continue doing it. What are not constructive are sarcastic comments that put down the writer or his/her material. I once took a writing class where we had one rule in reading each other's work: Be kind. I did not interpret this to mean that we couldn't be critical but to avoid being nasty or cruel."

In addition to asking teachers to reflect on their reactions to and preferences for feedback, we can also have them read and discuss the principles and processes of giving feedback delineated in Chapters 1–3. While we are discussing these principles in detail, we can share examples of feedback that illustrate these principles. To summarize:

1. Read first, with pencils down, and without any agenda.
2. Read again within the rhetorical context the writer has indicated on the cover note.
3. Respond to each writer and that writer's text individually; no two writers are the same and their needs and preferences will differ; no two texts are the same, so the needs of each writer will change from text to text.
4. Avoid overwhelming the writer by responding to everything. Choose what to respond to, considering the writer's rhetorical context, what the writer has indicated he/she would like feedback on, and what the major area is that stands in the way of the writer achieving his/her purpose for his/her audience.
5. Avoid appropriating the writer's text.
6. Point out what the writer is doing effectively.
7. Plan how to respond. Be text-specific, clear, direct; give revision strategies where warranted; use praise where warranted.

8. If this is a draft following a previous one, consider what the writer has revised. Respond to these revisions (with praise where warranted and with advice where warranted) and any concerns the writer has expressed about difficulties in revising or using your previous commentary.
9. Sum up your feedback in a way that the writer can learn from the feedback overall for this paper and for writing in general.

After these discussions, we can work with teachers on in-class activities that allow them to practice giving feedback by determining both what they might give feedback on and what they might say and how. In these activities, teachers can practice reading and responding to different texts that exhibit a range of issues that warrant feedback, different drafts of the same paper, different text types, and texts written by students at differing proficiency levels. By looking at a text exhibiting a number of issues that might warrant response, teachers can focus on prioritizing responses so that they do not overwhelm students. By examining a number of different texts, each with different types of problems, teachers can learn how to respond to a range of different issues, such as difficulties with organization, synthesis, overgeneralizations, writer-based prose, insufficient or inappropriate evidence, and so on. Responding to different text types allows teachers to see how feedback can be responsive to the unique combination of audience expectations, purpose, organization development, and language of particular text types. With practice on texts written by students at different levels of proficiency, teachers gain an understanding of how proficiency level affects exactly what we choose to respond to and how we word our responses to adjust to proficiency level. When teachers look at different drafts of the same paper written by one student, they can see how to read retrospectively, taking into account what the writer has or has not revised from the previous draft and what the writer needs help with in the current draft.

Because they do not know the students who wrote the texts on which we practice, it is important to preface the class practice work with descriptions that allow teachers to know about the student, the assignment, and the institutional context. (All my samples are from students I have taught in the past.) In this way, before they read and respond, they know who the audience is and what the student stated as the paper's purpose, they know the teacher's expectations for the assignment, and they know about the writing program. The intent is to mimic as best as possible the kinds of information they would have from a student's cover note and from working in a particular context.

I have found it helpful for teachers to work in small groups as they examine a range of texts and make decisions about what they will respond to and how. First, within the groups, they are able to provide a scaffold for each other. Second, they are able to hear different views about the texts, what needs feedback and why, and how to give this feedback. This is particularly informative and important because they begin to see that there may be different opinions about what to give feedback on and how. When we come back together as a whole class, we are able to discuss and compare the differences and similarities among our approaches, teasing out what differences are due to different readers, and what are more sound or less sound decisions and why.

Because teachers find responding to be difficult, one class session on responding is rarely sufficient enough time for practice, discussion, and the development of sound feedback practices. In my course on the teaching of writing, I allot several class sessions. In the first class, we discuss principles of feedback, look at illustrations of these principles in feedback to students' texts, and begin our practice on texts that display a range of problems. After this class, students do individual practice at home to which I respond (see pages 137–144 for a discussion of this practice and my responses). In the second class, we discuss their individual practice and my feedback to them, and they practice on more papers, this time also looking at more than one draft of the same paper. Oftentimes, we have a third session, after a second round of at-home practice, where we again discuss my feedback on their at-home practice and work on more responding in class. In all of these sessions, I ask them to share with me and their classmates what they find difficult and what successes they have had. These discussions allow us to address these difficulties so that they get help with whatever it is they feel they need help on.

Choosing Students/Texts for Individual Practice for Pre-Service Teachers

In addition to in-class work, teacher educators can also create individual assignments that will allow pre-service teachers to get practice with response and get feedback on their responses. The starting point for constructing these assignments is considering what second language composition students or what second language composition student texts teachers might work with. Since pre-service teachers are often not working with second language students, they do not have ready access to these students or their texts. Thus, one of the first questions to be answered is whether or not to have pre-service teachers work with actual students and their texts or just student texts.

Ideally, pre-service teachers would work with actual students, responding to their texts and helping these students with their writing. In this way, they could develop a sense of the student; the student's assignments; the context within which the student is learning and writing; the process of revision as the student writes, revises, and works with feedback; and how all these factors interact. If pre-service teachers will be working with students enrolled in L2 composition classes, it is important to get permission from the teacher of the writing class. In doing so, we need to be careful not to interfere with the normal workings of the writing class, thus asking the teacher to determine which writing assignments the pre-service teachers may work with, including which drafts. It is also important to work in a way that respects the due dates for the composition teacher's assignments, coordinating response assignment due dates to the writing class due dates. The pre-service teachers should share their responses with the composition teacher so that the composition teacher always knows what kind of feedback and help his/her students are getting from the pre-service teachers. Equally important is respecting the right of second language students to decide whether or not they want to participate; thus only those who volunteer would receive feedback from the pre-service teachers. Since it is important for pre-service teachers to understand how response fits within the whole context, it is preferable for them to attend some of the composition classes, to familiarize themselves with the syllabus and all of what the students will cover, and to familiarize themselves with the composition book (if one is used in the class) as well.

When pre-service teachers meet with their tutees (L2 writers) for the first time, they can do a needs analysis that allows them to get to know their tutees, in terms of the tutees' perceptions of their needs, perceptions of their strengths and weaknesses as writers, and their concerns and preferences for writing and feedback. These needs analyses allow pre-service teachers to find the most effective way to meet their tutees' needs and also allow us to address in our teaching of writing class the issues raised in Chapter 3 that are involved in addressing our second language students' needs and preferences for feedback.

Pre-service teachers need opportunities to see how second language writers' needs, difficulties, and progress change over the course of writing a paper and over the course of a semester. For this reason, they would also benefit from reading and responding to multiple drafts of the same paper as well as drafts of different papers written at different points in a semester.

Sometimes, however, we may find that there are no L2 writing classes available to our pre-service teachers, that some teachers may not want pre-service teachers giving feedback to their students, that some students may not want to work with pre-service teachers, or that timing works against us being able to coordinate the due dates for our assignments with the due dates for the writing assignments in the composition class. In these instances, pre-service teachers can work with texts that the teacher educator has collected from past second language writing students. In such situations, we can put together sets of papers so that our pre-service teachers see multiple drafts of one or more papers written by one student as well as that student's drafts of different papers written at different points in the semester. These selections would allow a teacher to get a sense of how one writer's work progresses over time within one paper and across papers and would come closest to working directly with one particular student. For example, in past courses, my teachers have chosen to "work" with one of three students and received that student's set of papers/drafts. Along with the set of papers, in order to come as close to real life as possible, teachers need information that they would have received if they were actually working with that student: the information that would be on the cover note prefacing each paper/draft, information about the student's preferences for feedback, information about the student's working "habits," information about the assignment, and information about the writing program.

The Response Assignment

Response assignments need to allow teachers to not only "practice" response but also to reflect on these responses and get feedback on their responses. To accomplish this practice, we can ask teachers to respond either to the actual students they are working with or to the sample papers we have given them as discussed previously. Practice, however, needs to be accompanied by careful reflection about what they are doing and why. This accomplishes several purposes: First, reflection pushes teachers to think about the choices they have made about what they are responding to and how they are responding—why they chose to respond to a particular aspect of the text but not to others, why they worded their responses in particular ways, what revision or writing strategies they offered their student and why, where they placed their commentary and why. Second, reflection allows the teacher educator to understand the teacher's decision-making processes and the reasons behind his/her decisions. Like the cover note second language writers give to their teachers, a written reflection accompanying a teacher's feedback allows the teacher educator to understand the teacher's agenda and respond accordingly.

To accomplish all of this, we can ask our teachers to start by coding their feedback (see Ferris, 2003; Ferris & Hedgcock, 1998) so they can see what they responded to and how. This allows them to notice and analyze patterns in their responses and reflect on what they feel is appropriate and what they might revise. Here is one example of the type of coding that teachers can do to analyze their comments.[2] While this coding covers all of the categories that teachers might analyze, teacher educators might adapt it so that they ask their teachers to focus only on particular elements within their commentary. Thus, teachers might look only at some of the columns, such as what they are commenting on or whether or not their comments are text-specific.

Analyzing Feedback

Analyze your comments in terms of **WHAT THEY FOCUS ON** (development, organization, writing process, audience expectations/needs, purpose, grammar, mechanics, lexical), **TONE** (praise, criticism, neutral tone), **DIRECTNESS** (direct, hedged), **FUNCTION** (ask for information, provide information, provide instruction, ask for revision, give instruction for revision, teachers correct or rewrite directly, direct student to do something other than revision [for example, read something], offer praise, offer criticism), **LINGUISTIC FORM** (question, statement, imperative, exclamation), and **TEXT SPECIFICITY** (text specific, non–text specific). Keep in mind that some comments might be coded for more than one characteristic within one category.

Comment #	What They Focus On	Tone	Directness	Function	Linguistic Form	Text Specificity
1						
2						
3						
4						
5						
6						
7						
8						

---

[2]This example is one I use with my teachers and is adapted from one my colleague John Hedgcock uses with his students.

After coding and analyzing their feedback, pre-service teachers can write a reflection that both describes and analyzes their feedback:

1. What principles from our class readings and class discussions guided what you responded to and how you responded?
2. What did you focus on as you responded to the student's paper? Why?
3. Describe the patterns you notice in each of the coding categories. Why did you decide to comment in the ways that you did? What do the results of your coding tell you about your feedback practices?
4. Given the patterns you see in your feedback, would you change anything in your responses?
5. What difficulties did you encounter as you planned your feedback and wrote your feedback?
6. What do you feel you need to practice and/or learn about to respond more effectively?[3]

The following example illustrates how a teacher's reflections addresses these questions and the coding of comments:

ED 560 Teaching of Writing 4/29/03

Reflection on My Response to Sonia's Second Draft

I found it much easier to respond to Sonia's second draft than to her first. To begin, I think my familiarity with both her essay and her writing abilities gave me a clearer idea of the direction my feedback should take. I almost feel like Sonia is my student now (it looks like I've "appropriated" her!). Another reason for this ease-of-response has to do with the improvements that Sonia made between the first and second drafts. In the second draft her ideas and argument are clearer, and so it was much easier to identify her purposes and tailor my comments to them. Most important, however, is the fact that the focused practice that responding

---

[3]Adapted from John Hedgcock, ED 560, class assignment, Monterey Institute of International Studies.

to the first draft gave me has combined with the insights I gained from the first reflection exercise to make me more confident about giving effective feedback. I also think that my knowledge and skill-set in this area have improved, too.

These increased levels of confidence, knowledge, and skill are reflected in the assumptions that guided my approach to Sonia's second draft. First of all, I retained the strategies that proved to be effective the first time around. Following Hyland and Hyland (2001), I once again tried to avoid mitigating my comments. As my data analysis shows, I was quite successful: Only five out of sixty comments are hedged, and of these five, most are only moderately hedged (i.e., I tend only to use "I think"). As a result I feel that my comments are much clearer and easier to "unpack." Further, I once again focused on the process instead of the product by giving summative comments that were future-oriented. In my response to Sonia's second draft I went even further: The first third of my summative comments concern the improvements that Sonia has made since her first draft. These comments, therefore, create linkages between the first, second, and third drafts and thereby underscore the multiplicity of the draft-writing process. I also again tried to avoid commenting on grammar while meaning still needed improvement (Ferris & Hedgcock 1998). I limited my comments on grammar (four out of a total of sixty) to areas where word use seriously interfered with meaning, a principle I also followed while responding to the first draft.

My analysis of my comments also shows me that I was more successful at applying some of my pre-planned strategies this time around. First and foremost, I again tried very hard to make as many of my comments as text-specific as possible. And, compared to my first-draft feedback, my second draft feedback shows a higher number of text-based directives, as well as a greater degree of explicit detail about what exactly it is that I'm asking Sonia to do. I also followed a principle that I learned in my Teaching of Writing seminar: Avoid appropriating the student's text by structuring comments as "if/ then" statements. I feel that by delivering most of my critical comments as "If you mean X, then do Y", I have given Sonia options for specific improvements instead of just telling her what to change. I was also much more successful at avoiding the use of questions while giving this second round of feedback (Hyland & Hyland 2001). This is arguably the biggest difference between my first and second-draft feedback, and I feel that Sonia will have a much easier time of putting my comments to productive use when she writes her third draft.

Although I feel pretty good about this newest set of comments, I can still see some areas that need improvement. When I look at my feedback as a whole, I am somewhat alarmed at the sheer volume of writing that I produced; I may very well have written more than Sonia! I cannot help but worry that writing too much could easily overwhelm a student --or even worse, result in discouragement. I also see an imbalance between positive and negative comments. I think I should have made striking a better balance here one of my guiding principles at the outset. Striking such a balance, then, will be at the forefront of the guiding principles that I marshal before I sit down to comment on Sonia's third draft.

References

Ferris, D., & Hedgcock, J. (1998). *Teaching ESL composition: Purpose, process, and practice*. Mahwah, NJ: Lawrence Erlbaum.

Hyland, F., & Hyland, K. (2001). Sugaring the pill: Praise and criticism in written feedback. *Journal of Second Language Writing, 10*, 185–212.

Giving Teachers Feedback on Their Written Responses

When teachers hand in their student's text with their feedback and their coding and reflections, the teacher educator then has a full picture of the teachers' feedback to their second language writers. We can see what they did (the feedback) and why (the reflection) and what they feel they need help with. This allows us in turn to provide optimal feedback to our teachers on their feedback. Because every reader of a text interacts with that text differently, it is essential that teacher educators know not only what their teachers responded to and how but *why* (Goldstein, 2002). Before I realized this, when I would read my teachers' feedback, I would sometimes find myself appropriating their responses. Some would tell me as much, saying that I wanted them to write a response that was *mine* rather than *theirs*. At first I didn't understand, and when this happened, I chalked this up to the difference between my expertise versus their lack of experience. However, once they began to explain to me how they had read the text they were commenting on and what decisions they had made and why, I began to see that sometimes it was not a difference of experience but a difference of how we interacted with the text—that is, how we had read and understood it. Thus, once I knew how they had read and understood a text and I understood their decisions, I could see whether decisions I would have made differently about what or how to respond were due to my greater expertise or because we had just read the text differently. One of my teachers, Karen, for example, wasn't sure what her student Dang was trying to do in his paper and that part of the difficulty discerning Dang's purpose was his use of transitions between paragraphs. When I read Dang's paper, I didn't have the same difficulty, but on seeing Karen's comments and her reflection, I could understand why she read Dang's paper the way that she did and why she commented the way that she did. So, although my reading was different, and my comments would have been different, I commented to Karen that given her reading, which she clearly explained to Dang, her comments were appropriate and effective.

Once we understand what our teachers choose to respond to and how they choose to respond and why, we have a context within which we can respond to their feedback, pointing out its strengths and its weaknesses. Thus, where we see that given how the teachers have read the text, their responses make sense, we can point out the soundness of their responses and also offer alternative interpretations of the text and alternative responses. In the previous example, I could offer Karen an alternative reading and explain how I would respond while simultaneously letting her know that her reading is also appropriate and her feedback to Dang appropriate and effective.

In contrast, where teachers' responses are not sound, even within the context within which they have read the paper, we can offer alternative sound responses When Chris commented in his cover note that "I originally felt that I should comment directly on the type of evidence he is putting forward, but after group discussions, I came to feel that I should not get too carried away and give the student too much advice," I replied that "I think this does need to be commented on. Since his goal is to demonstrate that job discrimination against minorities exists, his details need to be convincing that discrimination took place because of his ethnicity." Where Amy told her student Jan "great use of evidence and support for your points," I offered two pieces of advice. First, I told Amy that "since one of your concerns is teaching what makes support appropriate (good) here would be a good place to tell her *which* support is effective and *why.*" I also pointed out that "some of her (Jan's) support is not appropriate. For example, using outdated statistics to show that discrimination still exists" (Jan had used statistics from the beginning of the 1980s as well as from the 1920s to make a point about women's underrepresentation in politics in the mid- to late 1980s).

In addition, we can comment on patterns we see in their coding, pointing out patterns that suggest sound practices and patterns that suggest practices that need to be revised. Malika commented in her cover note that she "sought every opportunity to make my text-based feedback serve as a teaching tool. I tried to use summative feedback to explain to the student my comments instead of just saying that this is good or I don't understand this." In reading her commentary and looking at her coding, I could see that she had achieved this, and I commented, "Your feedback is text-specific, it explains why the areas commented on need revision, and it offers revision suggestions." In contrast, I could see from Chris's commentary and his coding that he was having difficulty with text-specific commentary. For example, he wrote in his commentary to his student "second paragraph: This paragraph is long and seems to fulfill more than one function. You might consider breaking it up into two paragraphs." I commented, "Let him know what two functions you see it fulfilling. It's "function" that would argue for revision into two paragraphs, something he won't be able to see without text-specific feedback." Furthermore, only five out of nine of Chris's comments were coded as text-specific, indicating that he needed to look at the four general comments and make them clearer and more explanatory by rewriting them as text-specific. In addition to giving him advice about how to make each comment text-specific, my end comment to him suggested, "Commentary needs to be text-specific and explanatory. That is, in order to help students understand our comments, we need to use text specificity to show exactly what part of the text we are referring to," letting Chris know that through text specificity we can let the student know what the problem is and why.

Furthermore, we can respond to what teachers have indicated they had difficulty with and what they feel they need help with or need to learn. Donna wrote in her cover note "I also tried to be more text-specific, even though the concept seems a bit vague and undefined to me. If I were a student and my teacher wrote, 'very clear title!' I would assume that my title was clear because it introduced the topic. Yet, on Sonia's paper, I made sure to write, 'Very clear title—it tells the reader which aspect of discrimination you will discuss,' just to be text-specific. In this particular case, I don't fully understand how the more text-specific comment is more meaningful than the more general comment." Donna's comment in her cover note allowed me to address her concern. I wrote back that if Donna's teacher commented "Very clear title" on her paper, the assumption that the teacher meant it was clear because it introduced the topic wasn't necessarily correct: "Maybe that's not why the teacher thought it was clear, i.e.,…the student doesn't have any idea what the teacher meant or the student comes up with a reason completely different from the one the teacher has."

In sum, the goal is to educate teachers about effective commentary by showing them where their feedback is effective and where it is less effective and why, by teaching how to make feedback more effective through comments on how to revise their feedback, and by responding to their questions and concerns. The teachers' coding and reflections allow them to learn on their own while providing teacher educators with a framework within which they can respond to the teachers' commentary.

In-Service Teachers: Learning about Response while Teaching

While supervising in-service teachers, I would regularly observe their classes, discussing with them the strengths of their teaching, what they would like to change in their teaching, and what I felt they could strengthen in their teaching.

Only over time did I realize that I was missing a central part of their teaching: their written feedback to their second language writers. Because so much individual instruction takes place through this feedback, it is important that supervisors of second language writing teachers expand their notions of observation and in-service education to include working with in-service teachers on their written responses.

Ideally, in-service teachers would participate in all of the tasks discussed previously for pre-service teacher education. They would have workshops to discuss product and process and workshops to discuss principles of giving feedback, and they would participate in practice feedback sessions. They would then code their responses to a few of their students and write reflections. After this, they would receive feedback from their supervisors in the same ways as discussed for pre-service teachers. They could then have more opportunities for feedback on their responses, as they refine and improve their practices.

However, teacher educators will need to consider in-service teachers' working conditions and how much time they can be asked to allot to in-service education. In particular, part-time instructors as well as full-time instructors with inordinately high teaching loads and large classes may not be able to participate in all of these activities. When faced with these circumstances, supervisors might ask in-service teachers to select some of their student papers and their commentary on these papers on which they would like to receive feedback and to indicate exactly what their concerns are and what they would like feedback on. They might attach a brief cover note, letting the supervisor know what they choose to give feedback on, how, and why and what they feel uncertain about. However, they would not necessarily code their feedback nor write a reflection, although they could be given a choice to code, if they wanted, for one or two particular characteristics. Depending on the supervisor's time constraints and workload, the supervisor could code the teachers' feedback in order to point out patterns or could selectively code for particular characteristics. In addition, over time, the supervisor could work with the teachers on all of the characteristics, one by one.

Summary

The following chart summarizes the steps teacher educators might take with their teachers to help them learn to provide effective written commentary to their second language writers. Each teacher educator will need to consider his or her setting and the teachers with whom he/she is working to make final decisions about the steps to undertake.

	PRE-SERVICE TEACHERS	**IN-SERVICE TEACHERS**
PREPARATION	Discuss writing processes and writing products	(If feasible)
	Keep track of and reflect on own writing processes	(If feasible)
	Analyze writing "products" from different discourse communities	(If feasible)
	Reflect on own attitudes toward and preferences for written feedback	(If feasible)
	Discuss principles of responding	Discuss principles of responding
PRACTICE	Teachers practice responding as a group	
	Teachers practice responding individually	Teachers respond to their own students
REFLECTION	Teachers code responses	(If possible; teacher educator might code responses)
	Teachers reflect on responses	(If feasible)
FEEDBACK	Teacher educator gives feedback to teachers on their responses	Supervisor gives feedback to teachers on their responses

Two themes have run consistently throughout this chapter and those that have preceded it, *complexity* and *communication*. Beginning with Chapter 1, we can see how complex the processes of teacher written feedback and student revisions are. All of the chapters speak to this complexity and argue for teachers, teacher educators, and researchers to examine carefully all of the factors that can affect how teachers give written commentary and how students work with their teachers' commentary. Within this complexity, communication is paramount. Teachers need to communicate clearly and consistently with their students about all facets of writing, revision, and working with commentary, and in turn they need to create the space, time, and means for students to communicate with them. Teachers and researchers can learn much from each other through communicating about their practices and findings, and we will all benefit through teachers' sharing what they learn from their reflective practices.

In sum, this book is the culmination of many conversations over the years—with my L2 writing students, with fellow teachers, with fellow researchers, and with my graduate students—conversations from which I have learned tremendously about the processes of teacher written commentary and student revision.

References

Anglada, L. (1995). On-line writing center responses and advanced ESL students' writing: An analysis of comments, students' attitudes and textual revisions. (Doctoral dissertation, Texas Tech University, 1995). *Dissertation Abstracts International, 60 (04A),* 1111.

Arias, R. (1995). The teacher as researcher: Action research revisited. *College ESL, 5,* 62–75.

Arndt, V. (1993). Response to writing: Using feedback to inform the writing process. In M. Brock & L. Walters (Eds.), *Teaching composition around the Pacific Rim: Politics and pedagogy* (pp. 90–116). Adelaide: Multilingual Matters.

Bailey, K. (1997). Reflective teaching: Situating our stories. *Asian Journal of English Language Teaching, 7,* 1–19.

Bailey, K., Bergthold, B., Braunstein, B., Fleischman, N., Holbrook, M., Tuman, J., et al. (1996). The language learner's autobiography: Examining the "apprenticeship of observation." In D. Freeman & J. C. Richards (Eds.), *Teacher learning in language teaching* (pp. 11–29). Cambridge: Cambridge University Press.

Benesch, S. (2001). Critical pragmatism: A politics of L2 composition. In T. Silva & P. Matsuda (Eds.), *On second language writing* (pp. 161–172). Mahwah, NJ: Lawrence Erlbaum Associates.

Brice, C. (1995). *ESL writers' reactions to teacher commentary: A case study.* (ERIC Document Reproduction Service No. ED394312)

Burke, B. (2004, April 26). Helping the needy crack the tax code. *Newsweek,* 16.

Canagarajah, A. S. (2002). *Critical academic writing and multilingual students.* Ann Arbor: University of Michigan Press.

Chapin, R., & Terdal, M. (1990). *Responding to our response: Student strategies for responding to teacher written comments.* (ERIC Document Reproduction Service No. ED328098)

Charles, M. (1990). Responding to problems in written English using a student self-monitoring technique. *ELT Journal, 44,* 286–293.

Cheong, L. K. (1994). Using annotation in a process approach to writing in a Hong Kong classroom. *TESL Reporter, 27,* 63–73.

Chi, F. (1999). *The writer, the teacher, and the text: Examples from Taiwanese EFL college students.* (ERIC Document Reproduction Service No. ED442272)

Cohen, A. (1991). Feedback on writing: The use of verbal report. *Studies in Second Language Acquisition, 13,* 133–159.

Cohen, A., & Cavalcanti, M. (1990). Feedback on written compositions: Teacher and student verbal reports. In B. Kroll (Ed.), *Second language writing: Research insights for the classroom* (pp. 155–177). Cambridge: Cambridge University Press.

Conrad, S., & Goldstein, L. (1999). ESL student revision after teacher written comments: Texts, contexts and individuals. *Journal of Second Language Writing, 8,* 147–180.

Cooper, M. (1986). The ecology of writing. *College English, 48,* 364–375.

Crawford, J. (1992). Student response to feedback strategies in an English for academic purposes program. *Annual Review of Applied Linguistics, 15,* 45–62.

Dessner, L. (1991). English as a second language college writers' revision responses to teacher-written comments. (Doctoral dissertation, University of Pennsylvania, 1991). *Dissertation Abstracts International, 52 (03A),* 827.

Ede, L. & Lundsford, A. (1984). Audience addressed/audience invoked: The role of audience in composition theory and pedagogy. *College Composition and Communication, 35,* 155–171.

Enginarlar, H. (1993). Student response to teacher feedback in EFL writing. *System, 21,* 193–204.

Faigley, L. (1986). Competing theories of process: A critique and a proposal. *College English, 48,* 527–542.

Ferris, D. R. (1995). Student reactions to teacher response in multiple-draft composition classrooms. *TESOL Quarterly, 29,* 33–53.

Ferris, D. R. (1997). The influence of teacher commentary on student revision. *TESOL Quarterly, 31,* 315–339.

Ferris, D. R. (1998, March). *How does teacher feedback affect student revision? A pilot comparison between ESL and NES writing teachers and their students.* Paper presented at the 32nd Annual TESOL Convention, Seattle, WA.

Ferris, D. R. (1999). One size does not fit all: Response and revision issues for immigrant student writers. In L. Harklau, K. Losey, & M. Siegal (Eds.), *Generation 1.5 meets college composition* (pp. 143–157). Mahwah, NJ: Lawrence Erlbaum Associates.

Ferris, D. R. (2001). Teaching writing for academic purposes. In J. Flowerdew & M. Peacock (Eds.), *Research perspectives on English for academic purposes* (pp. 298–324). Cambridge: Cambridge University Press.

Ferris, D. R. (2002). *Treatment of error in second language student writing.* Ann Arbor: University of Michigan Press.

Ferris, D. R. (2003). *Response to student writing: Implications for second language students.* Mahwah, NJ: Lawrence Erlbaum Associates.

Ferris, D. R., & Hedgcock, J. S. (2004). *Teaching ESL composition: Purpose, process, and practice (2d ed.).* Mahwah, NJ: Lawrence Erlbaum Associates.

Ferris, D. R., Pezone, S., Tade, C., & Tinti, S. (1997). Teacher commentary on student writing: Descriptions and implications. *Journal of Second Language Writing, 6,* 155–182.

Flower, L. (1979). Writer-based prose: A cognitive basis for problems in writing. *College English, 41,* 19–37.

Flower, L. & Hayes, J. (1981). A cognitive process theory of writing. *College Composition and Communication, 32,* 365–387.

Goldstein, L. (2001). For Kyla: What does the research say about responding to ESL writers. In T. Silva & P. Matsuda (Eds.), *On second language writing* (pp. 73–90). Mahwah, NJ: Lawrence Erlbaum Associates.

Goldstein, L. (2002, April). *Issues in preparing teachers of ESL writing.* Paper presented at the Thirty-Sixth Annual TESOL Convention, Salt Lake City, UT.

Goldstein, L., & Conrad, S. (1990). Input and the negotiation of meaning in ESL writing conferences. *TESOL Quarterly, 24,* 443–60.

Goldstein, L., & Kohls, R. (2002, April). *Writing, commenting and revising: The relationship between teacher feedback and student revision online.* Paper presented at the American Association of Applied Linguistics Conference, Salt Lake City, UT.

Grabe, W., & Kaplan, R. B. (1996). *Theory and practice of writing.* New York: Longman.

Greenhalgh, A. M. (1992). Voices in response: A postmodern reading of teacher response. *College Composition and Communication, 43,* 401–410.

Hairston, M. (1982). The winds of change: Thomas Kuhn and the revolution in the teaching of writing. *College Composition and Communication, 33,* 181–207.

Harris, M. (1989). Composing behaviours of one- and multi-draft writers. *College English, 51,* 174–191.

Hedgcock, J., & Lefkowitz, N. (1994). Feedback on feedback: Assessing learner receptivity in second language writing. *Journal of Second Language Writing, 3,* 141–163.

Hedgcock, J., & Lefkowitz, N. (1996). Some input on input: Two analyses of student response to expert feedback in L2 writing. *Modern Language Journal, 80,* 287–308.

Hyland, F. (1998). The impact of teacher written feedback on individual writers. *Journal of Second Language Writing, 7,* 255–286.

Hyland, F. (2000). ESL writers and feedback: Giving more autonomy to students. *Language Teaching Research, 4,* 33–54.

Hyland, F., & Hyland, K. (2001). Sugaring the pill: Praise and criticism in written feedback. *Journal of Second Language Writing, 10,* 185–212.

Hyland, K. (2003). Genre-based pedagogies: A social response to process. *Journal of Second Language Writing, 12,* 17–29.

Hyland, K. (2004). *Genre and second language writing.* Ann Arbor: University of Michigan Press.

James, C., & Garrett, P. (1991). The scope of language awareness. In C. James & P. Garrett (Eds.), *Language awareness in the classroom* (pp. 3–20). London: Longman.

Johns, A. (2002). *Genre in the classroom: Multiple perspectives.* Mahwah, NJ: Lawrence Erlbaum Associates.

Krapels, A. (1990). An overview of second language writing process research. In B. Kroll (Ed.), *Second language writing: Research insights for the classroom* (pp. 37–56). Cambridge: Cambridge University Press.

Krashen, S. D. (1984). *Writing: Research, theory and application.* Oxford: Pergamon Press.

Leki, I. (1990). Coaching from the margins: Issues in written response. In B. Kroll (Ed.), *Second language writing: Research insights for the classroom* (pp. 57–68). Cambridge: Cambridge University Press.

Leki, I. (1993). Reciprocal themes in ESL reading and writing. In J. Carson & I. Leki (Eds.), *Reading in the second language classroom: Second language perspectives* (pp. 9–32). Boston: Heinle and Heinle.

Lipp, E. (1995). Training ESL teachers to write effective feedback on composition drafts. *Journal of Intensive English Studies, 9,* 50–66.

Liu, J., & Hansen, J. (2002). *Peer response in second language writing classrooms.* Ann Arbor: University of Michigan Press.

Mlynarczyk, R. W. (1996). Finding grandma's words: A case study in the art of revising. *Journal of Basic Writing, 15,* 3–22.

Paulus, T. M. (1999). The effect of peer and teacher feedback on student writing. *Journal of Second Writing, 8,* 265–289.

Pennycook, A. (2001). *Critical applied linguistics.* Mahwah, NJ: Lawrence Erlbaum Associates.

Pratt, E. (1999). A qualitative study of peer and teacher response in an ESL writing classroom in Puerto Rico. (Doctoral dissertation, Indiana University of Pennsylvania, 1999). *Dissertation Abstracts International, 60 (02A),* 410.

Prior, P. (1991). Contextualizing writing and response in a graduate seminar. *Written Communication, 8,* 267–310.

Radecki, P., & Swales, J. (1988). ESL student reaction to written comments on their work. *System, 16,* 355–365.

Raimes, A. (1985). What unskilled ESL students do as they write: A classroom study. *TESOL Quarterly, 19,* 229–257.

Ramanathan, V., & Kaplan, R. (2000). Genres, authors, discourse communities: Theory and application for (L1 and) L2 writing instruction. *Journal of Second Language Writing, 9,* 171–191.

Reid, J. (1993). Historical perspectives on writing and reading in the ESL classroom. In J. Carson & I. Leki (Eds.), *Reading in the second language classroom: Second language perspectives* (pp. 9–32). Boston: Heinle and Heinle.

Reid, J. (1994). Responding to ESL students' texts: The myths of appropriation. *TESOL Quarterly, 28,* 272–292.

Richards, J., & Lockhart, G. (1994). *Reflective teaching in second language classrooms.* Cambridge: Cambridge University Press.

Rose, M. (1980). Rigid rules, inflexible plans, and the stifling of language: A cognitivist analysis of writer's block. *College Composition and Communication, 31,* 389–401.

Saito, H. (1994). Teachers' practices and students' preferences for feedback on second language writing: A case study of adult ESL learners. *TESL Canada Journal, 11,* 46–70.

Severino, C. (1998). The political implications of responses to second language writing. In T. Smoke (Ed.), *Adult ESL: Politics, pedagogy, and participation in classroom and community programs* (pp. 185–208). Mahwah, NJ: Lawrence Erlbaum Associates.

Sperling, M. (1994). Constructing the perspective of teacher-as-reader: A framework for studying response to student writing. *Research in the Teaching of English, 28,* 175–207.

Swales, J. (1990). *Genre analysis.* Cambridge: Cambridge University Press.

Zamel, V. (1983). The composing processes of advanced ESL students: Six case studies. *TESOL Quarterly, 17,* 165–187.

Zamel, V. (1985). Responding to student writing. *TESOL Quarterly, 19,* 79–102.

Subject Index

appropriation: avoiding through communication, 28; avoiding through reading students' annotations, 104; contextualizing of, 26; differentiating from effective intervention, 26–27; due to not understanding a text's audience or purpose, 27–28; recognizing and avoiding, 27; resulting from the teacher's status and power, 28; strengthening student intentions through commentary, 28. *See also* intervention

autobiographies: deriving student feedback preferences and strategies from, 50, 54

commentary. *See* teacher commentary

context (of writing, commenting, revising): accommodating program constraints, 15, 22–25; assessing institutional and programmatic attitudes and constraints, 10 (fig. 1), 13–14, 16–17; assessing student characteristics, 10 (fig. 1), 18, 22–25; assessing teacher characteristics and orientation, 10 (fig. 1), 18, 22–25; avoiding appropriation through communication, 28; commentary and revision as cyclical processes, 24–25; and critical pedagogy, 16; differentiating appropriation from intervention, 26–27; effects on multilingual students, 9–13, 22–25; effects on teachers, 9–12, 15–17, 22–25; effects on the quality of commentary, 11, 12–13, 22–25; how institutional and programmatic attitudes

affect teachers and students, 9–12, 13–14, 15–16, 22–25, 118; how institutional support (or its lack) affects writing programs, 11, 15–16, 22–25; how program requirements affect commentary and revision, 12, 15–16, 22–25; how teacher–student interactions affect commentary and revision, 19–25; and institutional attitudes toward minorities, 12–13, 15–16; modifying program constraints, 15, 16–17; no single standard context, 122–123; and not taking over a student's authorship, 19; students modifying their expectations, 21; teacher articulation of a "theory" of commentary, 20; teachers and rhetorical contexts, 39; teachers conducting a needs analysis with students, 21; teachers modifying their practices, 21; understanding the full context of a research study, 122–123

cover sheets, 36–39; example of, used in a graduate writing course, 67–68; example of, written for a descriptive essay, 37; example of, written for a sociology essay, 38; student miscommunicating his/her purpose on, 77; teacher development of, 39; using for student annotations and feedback requests, 67–69

feedback. *See* teacher commentary

first language writing. *See* L1 writing

Generation 1.5, 12, 15, 17, 37, 42

institutional attitudes. *See* context
intervention: differentiating appro-
    priation from effective intervention,
    26–27; strengthening student inten-
    tions through appropriate commen-
    tary, 28; teacher's responsibility to
    intervene with commentary, 39; text
    analysis fostering student–teacher
    communication, 28–29; *See also* ap-
    propriation

L1 writing: paradigm shift in, 2
L2 literature: and "process" approaches
    to writing, 2
L2 writers. *See* multilingual student
    writers

multilingual student writers: address-
    ing and accommodating program
    constraints, 15, 16–17, 22–25; appro-
    priating a text without understand-
    ing its audience or purpose, 27–28;
    assessing student characteristics, 10
    (fig. 1), 18, 22–25; benefits of full-class
    and small-group discussions, 35–36;
    benefits of teachers discussing process
    with students, 85–86; commentary as
    confusing or not helpful to students,
    40–41; conferences for discussing
    feedback and revisions, 57–58, 59
    chart; context and its effects on stu-
    dents, 9–13, 22–25; deriving feedback
    preferences from autobiographies and
    questionnaires, 50, 51–54; differentiat-
    ing appropriation from effective inter-
    vention, 26–27; discovering students'
    areas of textual concern, 61; effects
    of institutional and programmatic at-
    titudes on, 9–12, 13–14, 15–16, 22–25;
    effects of indirectness and mitiga-
    tion on, 96–97; how factors outside
    commentary affect students' use of
    feedback, 105; how teacher–student
    interactions affect commentary and
    revision, 19–25; and institutional
    attitudes toward minorities, 12–13,
    15–16; language awareness among,
    5–6; matching student and teacher
    preferences toward commentary,
    54–55; mischaracterizing students and
    their intentions, 57; modifying student
    expectations, 21; and peer feedback,
    6; providing feedback on writing
    processes, 84–85; reasons for unsuc-
    cessful revision, 55–57; response
    attitudes and strategies summarized,
    100, 101 chart; student confusion and
    mistrust over commentary, 41–42, 43;
    students' annotations of their texts, 39;
    students' differing preferences toward
    teacher feedback, 47–50; students'
    misinterpretations of "how" and
    "why" questions, 105; students and
    rhetorical contexts, 39; students work-
    ing with other students' texts, 31–32,
    33, 35; teacher commentary ignored or
    misused by, 4; on teachers conducting
    a needs analysis with students, 21; on
    teachers not taking over student au-
    thorship, 19; teaching students how to
    interpret and use commentary, 43–44,
    45, 46–47; textbooks available for, in
    1977, 1; uncovering students' prefer-
    ences regarding feedback, 50–51,
    62–63; using cover sheets for student
    annotations and feedback requests,
    67–69; using students' revision jour-
    nals, 115–116

programmatic attitudes. *See* context

questionnaires: deriving student feed-
    back preferences and strategies from,
    51–54; example of a feedback prefer-
    ences questionnaire, 52–54

reflective teaching: analyzing the in-
    teraction between commentary and
    revision, 114–115; author's personal
    lessons learned, 104–106; avoiding ap-
    propriation through reading students'
    annotations, 104; building a connec-
    tion among instruction, feedback, and
    revisions, 105; categorizing and coding
    revisions, 115; categorizing com-
    ments to identify one's own patterns,

107; changing one's typical patterns of commenting, 110–111; charting, coding, and analyzing one's own commentary, 112–114; contextualizing the notion of a successful revision, 115; counting the frequency of recorded comment types, 110; disseminating the findings of small-scale investigations, 119; experience and teacher growth, 103; and informed practice, 103; interviewing students to discover their uses of commentary, 116; and the L2 teaching field, 103; posing reflective questions on commenting and revising, 106; questions to aid teacher self-reflection, 117; reflecting on one's own patterns in commentary, 110; reflecting on which factors draw a teacher's comments, 106–107; reflection and "critical" analyses of teacher practices, 104; reflection leading to teacher self-awareness, 103–104, 117, 124; research into the forms taken by teachers' comments, 111–112; student annotations provoking reflection on commentary and revision, 104–105; students' misinterpretations of "how" and "why" questions, 105; text annotations as revealing the student's rhetorical context, 115; using coding charts to note student commentary, 107–109; using students' revision journals, 115–116
revision journals, 58, 59, 115–116, 125, 128

second language literature. See L2 literature
second language writers. See multilingual student writers
student annotations: avoiding appropriation through reading students' annotations, 104; as contributing to effective feedback and better revisions, 104; as encouraging students' critical reading of their texts, 104; as provoking reflection on commentary and revision, 104–105; text annotations as revealing

the student's rhetorical context, 115, 116; using cover sheets for, 67–69
student feedback. See teacher commentary
student writers cited: Bingo, 61–63, 81–82, 104; Chu Hua, 90–91; Dang, 142; Gin, 56; Hoshiko, 19–20, 22–25, 106; Jan, 90, 142–43; Jin, 70–71, 72–73; Lin, 65–66; Linh, 27–28, 32–33, 34–35; Marigrace, 105; Masaki, 78–80; Mei, 44–45, 83; Pilar, 69; Sam, 74–76, 89; Takara, 84–85; Thu, 64–65; Tranh, 84, 95–96, 105, 106; Zohre, 56, 105

teacher commentary: analyzing one's own composing processes, 126–128; analyzing the interaction between commentary and revision, 114–115; and think-aloud protocols, 85; appropriation due to the teacher's status and power, 28; appropriation due to not understanding a text's audience or purpose, 27–28; assessing comments for clarity, 97–98; avoiding appropriation through communication, 28; avoiding appropriation through reading students' annotations, 104; benefits of a "live" author explaining rhetorical strategies, 29; benefits of full-class and small-group discussions, 35–36; benefits of teachers discussing process with students, 85–86; building a connection among instruction, feedback, and revisions, 105; categorizing and coding revisions, 115; categorizing comments to identify one's own patterns, 107; changing one's typical patterns of commenting, 110–111; charting, coding, and analyzing one's own commentary, 112–114; commentary and revision as cyclical processes, 24–25; commentary with and without revision strategies, 98–100; compared to oral feedback through conferences, 7; comparing text-specific and non–text specific commentary, 92–94; conferences for discussing feedback and revisions, 57–58, 59 chart; considering the form, phrasing, and style of commentary, 89–90, 92; considering the syntactic shape of comments, 94–97; considering the tone of comments, 98; considering where to place commentary, 90–92; contextual factors affecting commentary quality, 11, 12–13, 22–25; contextualizing the notion of a successful revision, 115; counting the frequency of recorded comment types, 110; deriving feedback preferences from autobiographies and questionnaires, 50, 51–54; determining what teachers should comment on, 69; differentiating appropriation from effective intervention, 26–27; discovering students' areas of textual concern, 61; effects of indirectness and mitigation on students, 96–97; examining patterns of organization and development in texts, 63–66; extent of teachers' responses to student writing, 88–89; fostering teacher–student communication through text analysis, 28–29; how factors outside commentary affect feedback use, 105; how program requirements affect commentary and revision, 12, 15–16, 22–25; how teacher–student interactions affect commentary and revision, 19–25; including feedback about revisions in commentary, 86–89; interviewing students on commentary use, 116; looking for patterns of composing problems across students, 98–99; looking retrospectively at students' previous drafts, 86; matching student and teacher preferences toward commentary, 54–55; mischaracterizing students and their intentions, 57; mismatch between the writer's purpose and text, 77–78; misunderstanding composing processes as linear and ordered, 125–126; need for commentary and student feedback, 4–6; never assuming the reasons behind revision difficulties, 106; posing reflective

questions on commenting and revising, 106; as possibly confusing or not helpful to students, 40–41; principles of how to give feedback, 132–133; process approaches to teaching and learning, 6; process differentiated from "expressionism," 126n; providing effective commentary to multilingual writers, 1; providing feedback on a paper's lack of coherence, 81–82; providing feedback on inappropriate supporting evidence, 78, 79–80; providing feedback on insufficient story details, 80–81; providing feedback on student writing processes, 84–85; raising language awareness among students, 5–6; reasons for unsuccessful student revisions, 55–57; recognizing and avoiding appropriation, 27; reflecting on which factors draw a teacher's comments, 106–107; relationship of commentary to peer feedback, 6; relationship of commentary to revision, 2–4; research into the forms taken by teachers' comments, 111–112; research on, since 1990s, 3–4; research questions related to composing, commentary, and revision, 117–119; responding as both teachers and readers to student content, 82–83; responding to a mismatch between stated purpose and text, 74, 76, 77; responding to sentence-level communication difficulties, 69–70, 74; responding to sentence-level versus text-level issues, 69; responding to text-level problems of writer-based prose, 70–72, 74; responding with genuine praise in commentary, 83; response attitudes and strategies summarized, 100, 101 chart; strengthening student intentions through commentary, 28; student annotations of their texts, 39; student annotations provoking reflection on commentary and revision, 104–105; student confusion and mistrust over commentary, 43; student difficulties in using com-

mentary, 41–42; students' differing attitudes toward teacher feedback, 47–50; students' misinterpretations of "how" and "why" questions, 105; students' self-reports of using commentary when revising, 4; on students working with short published articles, 29; student teachers' difficulties in providing commentary, 3; summary of steps for providing effective commentary, 146 chart; teacher articulation of a "theory" of commentary, 20; teachers' personal experiences of learning to write, 2; teachers and rhetorical contexts, 39; teachers as "expert" readers, 6; teachers conducting a needs analysis with students, 21; teachers examining their commenting behaviors, 45–46; teachers modifying their practices, 21; teaching issues related to rhetoric and content, 1–3; teaching students how to interpret and use commentary, 43–44, 45, 46–47; text annotations as revealing the student's rhetorical context, 115; uncovering students' preferences regarding feedback, 50–51, 62–63; understanding the "shapes" writing takes in discourse communities, 128–130; using classroom discussions of commentaries, texts, and revisions, 46–47; using coding charts to note student commentary, 107–109; using cover sheets for student annotations and feedback requests, 67–69; using cover sheets to communicate audience, intention, and point of view, 36–39; using students' revision journals, 115–116; what the teacher should respond to in student writing, 88; writing instruction given to student teachers, 2–3
teacher education for in-service teachers, 2, 3, 8, 27, 125, 147; activities for expanding in-service education, 145; analyzing one's own composing process, 126–128; difficulties in giving sound written feedback, 125, 128; discourse analysis of published work (class assignment), 129–130; expanding in-service education to include feedback responses, 144–145; how they might work with teacher educators, 125; misunderstanding composing processes as linear and ordered, 125–126; principles of how to give feedback, 132–133; process differentiated from "expressionism," 126n; summary of steps for providing effective commentary, 146 chart; understanding the "shapes" writing takes in discourse communities, 128–130
teacher education for pre-service teachers, 2, 3, 8, 27, 125, 147; analyzing one's own composing processes, 126–128; assignments for practicing and reflecting on teacher response, 137–138; coding and analyzing response feedback, 138; discourse analysis of published work (class assignment), 129–130; giving teachers feedback on their responses, 141–144; in-class practice at responding to different text types, 133–134; misunderstanding composing processes as linear and ordered, 125–126; personal reactions to feedback, 130–132; principles of how to give feedback, 132–133; process differentiated from "expressionism," 126n; summary of steps for providing effective commentary, 146 chart; their difficulties in giving written feedback, 125, 128; understanding the "shapes" writing takes in discourse communities, 128–130; working in small groups to examine texts, 134–135; working with sample texts instead of actual students, 136–137; working with students on individual assignments, 135–136; working with teacher educators, 125; writing self-reflections that describe and analyze feedback, 139–141
teacher research, 3, 103; author's personal lessons learned, 104–106; avoiding confounding variables in research, 120; collecting sufficient data, 122; comparability across research studies,

123–124; disseminating the findings of small-scale investigations, 119, 124; methodological problems in research, 120–121; no single standard context, 122–123; research into the forms taken by teachers' comments, 111–112; research lacking on the relationship between commentary and revision, 114, 119, 124; research on commentary as lacking sufficient detail, 122–124; research questions on composing, commentary, and revision, 117–119; small-scale research studies and their value, 119, 124; understanding the full context of a research study, 122–123

teacher–student communication: addressing program constraints through teacher–student collaboration, 16–17; assessing student characteristics, 10 (fig. 1), 18, 22–25; assessing teacher characteristics and orientation, 10 (fig. 1), 18, 22–25; the benefits of full-class and small-group discussions, 35–36; benefits of teachers discussing process with students, 85–86; building a connection among instruction, feedback, and revisions, 105; conferences for discussing feedback and revisions,

57–58, 59 chart; deriving feedback preferences from autobiographies and questionnaires, 50, 51–54; discovering students' areas of textual concern, 61; the effects of indirectness and mitigation on students, 96–97; effect of institutional and programmatic attitudes affect on, 9–12, 13–14, 15–16, 22–25; how teacher–student interactions affect commentary and revision, 19–25; matching student and teacher preferences toward commentary, 54–55; mischaracterizing students and their intentions, 57; oral feedback (conferences) compared to commentary, 7; raising language awareness among students, 5–6; response attitudes and strategies summarized, 100, 101 chart; students' differing attitudes toward feedback, 47–50; students' misinterpretations of "how" and "why" questions, 105; students ignoring or misusing commentary, 4; on teachers conducting a needs analysis with students, 21; using classroom discussions of commentaries, texts, and revisions, 46–47

Zone of proximal development, 6

Author Index

Anglada, L., 40, 42, 48, 55
Arias, R. 117
Arndt, V., 40, 41, 42–43, 48

Bailey, K., 81, 103, 104
Benesch, S., 12, 16
Brice, C., 48

Canagarajah, A. S., 12, 16
Cavalcanti, M., 12, 48
Chapin, R., 28, 40, 42–43
Charles, M., 27
Cheong, L. K., 27
Chi, F., 18, 28, 40, 42–43
Cohen, A., 12, 40, 43, 48, 49
Conrad, S., 7, 19, 21, 27, 40, 42, 43, 46, 50, 55, 56, 84, 95, 96, 98, 99, 104, 114
Cooper, M., 126
Crawford, J., 40, 42–43

Dessner, L., 83

Ede, L., 5
Enginarlar, H., 48, 56

Faigley, L., 126
Ferris, D. R., 1, 3, 5, 21, 42–43, 47, 48, 49, 58, 69, 83, 90, 92, 95, 96, 97, 98, 99, 100, 138, 140, 141
Flower, L., 70, 85, 126

Garrett, P., 6
Goldstein, L., 4, 7, 9, 19, 21, 27, 40, 42, 43, 46, 50, 55, 56, 57, 84, 85, 95, 96, 98, 99, 104, 114, 117, 120, 141
Grabe, W., 6, 29, 36
Greenhalgh, A. M., 28

Hairston, M., 2
Hansen, J., 6
Harris, M., 126
Hayes, J., 85
Hedgcock, J., 5, 21, 48, 83, 90, 92, 138, 139, 140, 141
Hyland, F., 26, 28, 40, 43, 49, 83, 94, 96, 140, 141
Hyland, K., 40, 49, 56, 83, 94, 96, 126, 128, 140, 141

James, C., 6
Johns, A., 128

Kaplan, R. B., 6, 29, 36, 128
Kohls, R., 7, 19, 21, 40, 42–43, 50, 55, 56, 57, 85, 87–88, 99
Krapels, A., 126
Krashen, S. D., 4

Lefkowitz, N., 48
Leki, I., 4, 5, 26, 27, 40
Lipp, E., 83
Liu, J., 6
Lockhart, G., 103, 104
Lundsford, A., 5

Mlynarczyk, R. W., 27

Paulus, T. M., 43
Pennycook, A., 16
Pezone, S., 3
Pratt, E., 56
Prior, P., 18

Radecki, P., 3, 43, 45, 48, 49, 56
Raimes, A., 126

Ramanathan, V., 128
Reid, J., 5, 26, 27, 43
Richards, J., 103, 104
Rose, M., 126

Saito, H., 40
Severino, C., 12
Sperling, M., 118
Swales, J., 3, 43, 45, 48, 49, 56, 128–29

Tade, C., 3
Terdal, M., 27–28, 40, 42–43
Tinti, S., 3

Vygotsky, L., 6

Zamel, V., 3, 40, 126